The
Quest
for
Holiness
DAVID C. LONG

FROM CASUAL CONVICTION

TO COURAGEOUS FAITH

Printed in the United States of America

Cover design by Strange Last Name
Page design by PerfecType, Nashville, Tennessee

Long, David C. (David Clifton), 1951-
The quest for holiness : from casual conviction to courageous faith / David C. Long. – Franklin, Tennessee : Seedbed Publishing, ©2020.

pages ; cm.. + 1 videodisc – (Quest for holiness)

Includes bibliographical references
ISBN 9781628247664 (paperback)
ISBN 9781628247701 (DVD)
ISBN 9781628247671 (Mobi)
ISBN 9781628247688 (ePub)
ISBN 9781628247695 (uPDF)

1. Holiness--Christianity. 2. Spiritual formation 3. Christian life--Methodist authors. I. Title. II. From casual conviction to courageous faith.

BT767 .L665 2020 248.4 2020933068

SEEDBED PUBLISHING
Franklin, Tennessee
seedbed.com

Contents

The
Quest
for
Holiness
DAVID C. LONG

1

Setting Our Sights on Heaven

> *Can you trust Jesus Christ where your common sense cannot trust Him? Can you venture out with courage on the words of Jesus Christ, while the realities of your common-sense life continue to shout, "It's all a lie"? . . . Faith is absolute trust in God—trust that could never imagine that He would forsake us.*
>
> —Oswald Chambers

It was one of those rare, once-in-a-lifetime situations in which a person is called to take on a momentous task that seems impossible. The thought of running in the other direction would come naturally for most of us, but that was not an option. It was a calling that would put even great faith to the test. There are many times and many places throughout the Bible where this call to courageous faith may be found. This time, it was the command to Joshua when he was thrust into leadership at one of the most critical times in the history of the nation of Israel. After forty years in the wilderness under the leadership of Moses, Israel was at the banks of the Jordon River, on the verge of the conquest of the promised land. Imagine how Joshua must have felt, stepping into the shoes of the greatest leader in the history of Israel. Moses had confronted the powerful Pharaoh face-to-face and had led the Israelites out of bondage in Egypt. His résumé highlights included the parting of the Red Sea, meeting with God on Mt. Sinai, and the giving of the law. Now, with Moses gone, Joshua was appointed to be his successor and he was told to be strong and courageous.

Joshua had been prepared for this day, at least as far as one can be prepared for such a crucial role. He had been the trusted assistant of Moses, one of the twelve spies sent into the promised land years earlier. He had been in a position where he observed Moses and had been tutored for leadership. Now, the Israelites were entering a land promised to them but in which lived thirty-one kings bent on their destruction, and Joshua was Israel's leader. God's instruction to Joshua was straightforward and bold, "Be strong and courageous." He repeated the command with emphasis, "Be strong and very courageous." And in case Joshua was not hearing, "Be strong and courageous! Do not be afraid or discouraged. For the LORD your God is with you wherever you go" (Josh. 1:6–7, 9).

Be strong and courageous. It's easy for us to understand how these words of command and encouragement were appropriate for Joshua. We can readily apply them to King David as he built and defended the nation, and to the prophets of the Old Testament who fearlessly proclaimed the word of God to a rebellious people. These words certainly typify the attitude of the apostle Paul on his three missionary journeys, repeatedly staring death in the face. Examples continue down through the ages, including missionaries like William Carey and Amy Carmichael in

India, Hudson Taylor as he took the gospel message to the interior of China, and so many other notable heroes of faith. The question we are asking, though, is whether this is also a command to those of us who are, well, more ordinary Christians—to pastors, Sunday school teachers, and believers sitting in the pew? Are we also to live lives of strong and courageous faith?

There is an invitation that comes to all followers of Jesus. It's an invitation to think outside the box. This way of thinking is neither easy nor natural, since the box holds our attention captive, containing as it does all the seemingly important items of day-to-day life. But the effort is important. Peter Drucker was a management consultant, educator, and author who has been described as the founder of modern management. There is a story about a management seminar conducted by Drucker for which a group of executives paid handsomely to attend. Drucker began with a question, "What is the most essential thing for an executive to understand?" One executive proposed the market and marketing trends. Drucker acknowledged this as important, but not as the most important thing to understand. Others proposed the finances of the organization, management of people, and so on. Drucker acknowledged each as important, but of each he said it was not the answer he was seeking. Finally, one executive suggested that since they had paid so much money to hear from Drucker, perhaps *he* would tell them the answer. "The most important thing for an executive to understand," replied Drucker, "is reality!"

Reality! This was an unexpected answer! It would seem to have more to do with a philosophical discussion than a seminar on management. But the founder of modern management identified this as the understanding of ultimate importance. Understanding reality has an essential role in living with courageous faith as well. We live in the midst of many distractions that tend to keep us from seeing reality as clearly and completely as we need, that tend to keep our focus inside the box. Yet, an understanding of reality provides a true framework for the motivation and empowerment that fuels spiritual formation.* If this is true, then it reasonably follows that a deepening understanding of reality is an essential pursuit in our spiritual journey. This isn't drawn from principles of management, but from the Bible.

What is this reality that we as disciples of Jesus need to understand and, understanding, need to keep in focus in every facet of our life? One thing for certain, if understanding reality is important in business management, it is even more important in the management of our lives. As in Drucker's seminar, many answers are offered. There are many worldviews, but they are not consistent with each other and only one holds the truth. William Barclay has this reality in mind when he writes, "It is given to every man to live in two worlds, this world of space and time, and the world of eternal things. Our danger is that [we] become so involved in this world that we forget the other."[1] In other words, the danger is that our eyes become

---

*The primary work of sanctification in our life is that of the Holy Spirit, but we are called to participate through reading the Word, prayer, worship, and other means of grace. See chapters 5 and 6 of *The Quest for Holiness: From Shallow Belief to Mature Believer.*

fixed solely on those things inside the box (the world of space and time) without regard for the great reality outside the box (the world of eternal things).

C. S. Lewis writes about the soul-deadening power of a false perception of "real life" in *The Screwtape Letters*. Writing to his subordinate Wormwood, the more senior devil Screwtape says of humankind, "Thanks to the process we set at work in them centuries ago, they find it all but impossible to believe in the unfamiliar while the familiar is before their eyes."[2] The familiar makes it difficult for us to give serious regard to any thought that draws our mind away from everyday experiences.

It's easy to think that something good awaits at the end of this life, but not give much thought to what that really means here and now. This attitude prevails despite scriptures that tell us our life here on earth is like the morning fog, here a little while then it's gone (James 4:14) or like flowers that quickly wither and fade (Isa. 40:7). So here is the reality. As followers of Jesus saved by grace, we do not have two lives, one in this world and one later in heaven. Rather we have one continuous everlasting life. As we are able to apply this understanding, we see the wonderful certainty that each day of our life is connected to and has meaning throughout our eternal existence.

When we, by grace, understand the breadth of this reality, it should motivate us to live accordingly. It can free us to grow in Christlike faith and to live out our faith in God more fully and completely. We are empowered to move from a life of casual conviction to courageous faith. Jesus encouraged this view toward everlasting life when he instructed, "but store up for yourselves treasures in heaven, where neither moth nor rust consumes and where thieves do not break in and steal" (Matt. 6:20 NRSV). He gives us a template for the priorities of our life saying, "But strive first for the kingdom of God and his righteousness, and all these things will be given to you as well" (Matt. 6:33 NRSV). Paul seems to have had this in mind when he wrote to the Philippians, "But we are citizens of heaven, where the Lord Jesus Christ lives" (Phil. 3:20). More to the point, he admonished the Colossians, "Since you have been raised to new life with Christ, set your sights on the realities of heaven . . ." (3:1). Do you hear the emphasis on the present reality of heaven in these verses? Think of heaven more as relationship with God than a place. These verses don't allow for a focus on the things of the world to the exclusion of things eternal.

It's not easy to think, much less live, outside the box, which holds the consuming influence of the visible, tangible world. This was evident in the early days of the church in a community of believers formed mainly of Jewish converts. Much remains uncertain about this community, including where it was located and who wrote the letter to them that we now know as the book of Hebrews. These believers were second-guessing their decision to leave the rituals of Judaism and follow Jesus. This seems to have been due in part to persecution, but we can also be sure that there was great pressure as they watched family, friends, and community continue the ancient rituals of Judaism. The temple in Jerusalem had not been destroyed when this letter was written, so the work of the priests, offering sacrifices for the sins of the people, continued around them day after day after day. This was their visible, tangible world. But they had professed faith in Jesus, the true High Priest, and in his sufficiency for their lives. Surrounded by a culture of inadequate ritual, they had been called to a life of faith. But doubts crept in, and they began to ask, "Have we made the right decision? Is this message of Jesus true? Can we really live by faith in Jesus?" In other words, were they really willing to live out the faith they professed? It wasn't wrong for this community to be asking these questions. Such questions are part of growing in Christlike faith. But as the questions are asked, it is of the utmost importance that the correct answers be found. Thinking outside the box brings us face-to-face with the question of what it really means to live a life of faith in the reality of the promises of God.

That's what we are called to, faith that transcends the world of space and time and an ever-deepening trust in the God of eternal things. This letter to this Hebrew community contains a very pointed criticism. They have been believers for some time, long enough that they should now be teachers. Instead, in their casual conviction, they are still like babies who must be fed milk, unable to handle solid food appropriate for mature believers (5:11–14). They were tempted by the falsehood and distraction around them to ignore things eternal. The author of the letter says, "Come on! It's time to grow up in Christ! Simple, basic truths such as putting aside salvation by self-help rituals and instead trusting Jesus have been taught to you time and time again. Don't be spiritually dull and indifferent. Rather, with God's help, it's time to go deeper and to grow more like Jesus, whom we proclaim as Savior" (Heb. 6:1–12, author's paraphrase). In other words, the time for casual conviction regarding the Christian life has passed. As the author of the letter says, God willing, our faith must grow deeper.

This is not about ignoring or minimizing this visible world as if we could live only in the eternal world. As is often repeated, we don't want to be so heavenly minded that we are of no earthly good. It's about accepting the present reality of both worlds and living our one life accordingly. It's accepting that we are living for eternity. J. C. Ryle served as a pastor for forty years before being appointed bishop of Liverpool in 1880. He wrote of the continuity between this life and life everlasting,

> Let no man deceive himself on this point. If anything is certain about the future, it is certain that there will be a judgment; and if anything is certain about judgment, it is certain that men's "works" and "doings" will be considered and examined in it (John 5:29; 2 Cor. 5:10; Rev. 20:13). He that supposes works are of no importance, because they cannot justify us, is a very ignorant Christian.[3]

In other words, beyond our justification (conversion), how we as Christians live this life has consequences in our future, our everlasting life! Likewise, that our lives are eternal has consequences in our present life. So, seek to live with an awareness of the reality of our everlasting life and let that awareness influence our actions in our daily life. If it is true that nothing should be considered as trivial because nothing in our lives is a mere insignificant detail to God, then we are talking about something pervasive, a way of living that embraces all of our lives. We, like the believers in Hebrews, ask the question, "Can this kind of faith be a part of our lives?" We cannot just flip a switch and turn from a life of casual conviction to one of Christlike faith, but God would not set us on such a journey without providing for us. This transformation is a work of the Holy Spirit and we commit to seeking and surrendering to this work through prayer, study of the Word, worship, encouraging fellowship in community, and other means of grace made available to us. We also have the benefit of observing the lives of others, saints whose stories are recorded in Scripture. We see their struggles, their questions, their answers, and are challenged and encouraged by them.

One of those heroes of faith is Abraham. Paul refers to Abraham as the father of all who believe (Rom. 4:16). This doesn't mean he was the first to believe, but that his faith had a quality that serves as a model for us. There's a good chance there is something to learn about faith from his life. One of the events in this remarkable life where we witness courageous faith is in the story of Abraham and Lot.*

Abraham was a son of Terah, who lived in Ur of the Chaldeans with his three sons. Terah began the journey to the land of Canaan, the promised land, but stopped in Haran where he died having abandoned the journey.

---

*In this story, our hero is still named Abram. His name has not yet been changed by God to Abraham, a change made along with the promise to give him countless descendants (Gen. 17:1–6).

The command passed to Abraham to leave his country, his relatives, and his father's family to "go to the land that I will show you" (Gen. 12:1).

> So Abram departed as the LORD had instructed, and Lot went with him. Abram was seventy-five years old when he left Haran. He took his wife, Sarai, his nephew Lot, and all his wealth—his livestock and all the people he had taken into his household at Haran—and headed for the land of Canaan. When they arrived in Canaan, Abram traveled through the land as far as Shechem. There he set up camp beside the oak of Moreh. At that time, the area was inhabited by Canaanites.
>
> Then the LORD appeared to Abram and said, "I will give this land to your descendants." And Abram built an altar there and dedicated it to the LORD, who had appeared to him. (Gen. 12:4–7)

Two things stand out in this story: the huge step of faith as Abraham undertook this journey, and God's promise to give this land to Abraham and his descendants. It would not have been lost on Abraham as he contemplated this promise that the promised land was inhabited by the Canaanites and that he had no descendants. His wife, Sarah, was well past the age of bearing children. But Abraham believed God.

Abraham was the patriarch at a time when the patriarch held all the rights of the family. The patriarch could rule with autocratic authority over his children and his children's children for as long as he lived. His word, his decision, was simply to be obeyed. Lot was Abraham's nephew, his father having died while the family was still in Ur. Both Abraham and Lot became very wealthy with flocks of sheep and goats, herds of cattle, and many tents. Lot's wealth likely would have been through the generosity of Abraham. In Genesis 13 we read that after a sojourn in Egypt, Abraham and Lot returned to the promised land, but the land could not support both of them with their flocks and herds so close together. Disputes broke out among the herdsmen. Which herd can graze where, and which could use which wells for water? These probably led to more serious disputes. Finally, it was Abraham who called for an end to the conflict. But to our surprise, he made an amazing offer to Lot. It certainly would have been Abraham's right to take the best of the land for himself, leaving what was left for Lot. Instead Abraham said to Lot: "The whole countryside is open to you. Take your choice of any section of the land you want, and we will separate. If you want the land to the left, then I'll take the land on the right. If you prefer the land on the right, then I'll go to the left" (Gen. 13:9).

Lot was immediately willing to accept this offer. Lot looked and saw the fertile Jordan Valley, well-watered like the garden of the Lord, or the beautiful land of Egypt (Gen. 13:10). He chose that land with no gratitude, no hesitation, and no concern. Abraham simply gave him his choice. What did Abraham know that freed him to make this unselfish gesture? What was there in Abraham's faith in God that freed him to make this offer? What was the substance of this faith? Lot based his decision on what appeared to him to be attractive, a logical choice without considering God's will beforehand. Abraham believed

God, but not just that God exists. Even the demons believe this (James 2:19). And not just that something wonderful awaited him at the end of his life. Abraham's faith meant that he believed his relationship with God hovered over, in, and through every action and aspect of his life. Abraham did not see God's provision then believe, he believed in confidence that he would see. He exchanged the confidence he might have had in himself as the patriarch for confidence in God. That is courageous faith. I wish we could see a picture of Abraham as he began to lead his family toward the less desirable land. I believe we would see a calm confidence on his face that assured the others that there was no need to ask why.

The progression from casual conviction to courageous faith is seen in the story of Jesus and his disciples. The gospel story has a pivot point with Peter's confession that Jesus is the Messiah (Matt. 16:16; Mark 8:29; Luke 9:20). This was also the point at which Jesus turned toward Jerusalem and the suffering to come, and when he began to teach his disciples what messiahship meant. Peter's confession was a wonderful start, but the disciples did not know what Jesus meant when he told them he must suffer and die, and on the third day would rise from the dead. The lesson on true messiahship had begun, but it would not be complete until after the cross and resurrection. The disciples didn't understand the full significance of Jesus healing those who came to him, quieting the wind, walking on water, and feeding the thousands. Indeed, when they talked about the coming kingdom they wondered which of them would be the greatest. Though beginning to recognize Jesus as Messiah, they were still looking for a leader who would fix their problems (casual conviction). Jesus wanted them to know him as the Messiah with whom they would journey through death and resurrection (courageous faith). The disciples needed to trust Jesus fully as sovereign, overcomer, King of kings, Lord of lords, and constant friend. After the cross, the disciples were fearful and were in hiding. After the resurrection, they were transformed into disciples with the courageous faith needed to carry forward the ministry of Jesus.

The bedrock of courageous faith is God. It's not in the quality of our faith, but in the nature of God. He designed us for everlasting life in an intimate, loving union with himself, the one we know as Father! This is the reality into which everything in our lives should fit. It is an amazing truth, but the natural state of our lives lacks full comprehension of this reality. We may know the words, but we have to work diligently at adjusting our vision and realigning our hearts to live by this reality. C. S. Lewis says failing to live in this truth is "like an ignorant child who wants to go on making mud pies in a slum because he cannot imagine what is meant by the offer of a holiday at the sea."[4]

Ignoring the present reality of everlasting life says grace settles believers' eternal destiny, which indeed it does, but it also says that not much more will happen until we get to heaven. "Our life on earth becomes more of a waiting room than an adventure or journey with God."[5] Thankfully, the promise of God to his children is transformation, a process in which we are becoming the person we are designed to be, fit for everlasting life. Do you let this truth, this promise, motivate you? Does it encourage and empower you? To do so is to think and live outside the box, to live in the place of courageous faith.

In answer to the question with which we began, we *are* to live as strong and courageous Christians. Casual conviction doesn't conquer our Jericho, nor does it guide our family in these tumultuous times. Very few among us face a task like that faced by Joshua or the many others who have helped to greatly advance the kingdom of God. Still, we miss a critically important point if we only attach the call to be strong and courageous to military prowess, missionary endeavor, or great feats of evangelism. Don't be casual about this! Remember how God has been faithful and set your heart deliberately on growing deeper in faith! Just as much as in the battles to conquer the land, courageous faith is about the commitment that whatever comes, we will serve the Lord. Courageous faith is not defined by the difficulty of the battle or the size of the task. Courageous faith is abandonment of self-interest, pride, and self-sufficiency. It is trusting God to make a holy experiment out of us.

Make a habit of constantly returning to an awareness of our everlasting relationship with our Lord. By grace through Jesus, we have the promise of everlasting life with our Father. We are to find the identity, meaning, value, and purpose of our lives in the context of this everlasting life, a reality that includes but is much greater than all we may encounter in this visible world. As we learn to live according to this principle, we will grow in our ability to truly love God and love our neighbor. In the following chapters we will consider how we might apply this principle to some of the challenges we face as

Christians. How might the habit of applying this affect us when facing dry seasons, suffering, or the challenges of forgiveness? How might we live differently if we grow in our ability to apply this principle in relationships with others within our community? This is part of our adventure with God.

A pastor who had a deep godly influence in my life often paraphrased the words of Phillips Brooks as a benediction.

> Do not pray for easy lives but rather pray to be strong men and women.
>
> Do not pray for a task equal to your power, but rather pray for power equal to your task.
>
> Then the doing of your work will be no miracle, but you will be the miracle!
>
> And you will be constantly amazed at what you can do and become by the grace of God through Jesus Christ living within you.
>
> Unto whom be glory and majesty, dominion and power, both now and forevermore.

Reflection and Application:

1. "No eye has seen, no ear has heard, and no mind has imagined what God has prepared for those who love him" (1 Cor. 2:9). What does this verse mean to you? How might a day lived with the awareness of eternal life change the way you act and think throughout that day?

2. In what area of your life of faith have you been strong and courageous? What equipped you for such faith? What is an area where you need to be strong and courageous? What does that look like? What is a step to be taken in that direction?

3. What is one thought you can take from this chapter to reflect upon in the days ahead with the guidance of the Holy Spirit? What is one prayer over which you will spend time with the Lord?

2

The Mistake of the Pharisees

Religious forms of self-improvement can also generate nervous self-concern and spiritual pride. If growth is built on repressed guilt, or if the means of growth is a set of laws to be followed or an intricate and arduous path to be mastered, spiritual self-centeredness will result.

—Richard F. Lovelace

For a follower of Jesus, the command for holiness describes the goal of his or her Christian life.* The message of Jesus and his disciples was not just one of accepting the free gift of salvation and waiting for heaven, but rather a message of newness of life and transformation now into a deeper relationship with our Father in heaven. We simply must not miss this relational aspect of our lives as Christ-followers. As Steve DeNeff writes, holiness "is an ever-increasing oneness [with God] prompted by love."[1] Yet, the topic of holiness has led to misunderstanding and confusion. Jesus leads us to a deeper understanding of

*Holiness is the focus of the three books in this series. This was the subject in chapter 4 of the first book, *The Quest for Holiness: From Shallow Belief to Mature Believer.*

holiness by showing us the difference between his way of living and that of the Pharisees. It stands to reason that reflection upon the lives of the Pharisees is one means of clarifying our understanding of holiness.

So, what understanding of holiness might we gain from looking at this group of people? For that matter, who are they? I recall visiting a synagogue as part of a seminary class on comparative religions. One of the comments made to our class by the rabbi was that Pharisees have really received a bad rap. They have been unfairly criticized! It's a sentiment that has been expressed many times over the years, so it's prudent that we understand who the Pharisees really were and for what they stood.

Today, the word *Pharisee* is generally used in a derogatory manner to describe someone who is self-righteous and hypocritical. That has not always been the case. In fact, in Jesus' time many people viewed the Pharisees with respect, the title as one of honor. They were an elite group among Jewish leaders! Even in the New Testament, while overall harshly critical of them, positive events can be found. On one occasion they warned Jesus of a scheme against him by King Herod (Luke 13:31). In Acts, we read that Gamaliel, a Pharisee who was a highly respected teacher, intervened on behalf of Peter and John when they were put on trial by the Jewish high council. Gamaliel persuaded the council to dismiss the charges against them (Acts 5:33–39). Pharisees also came to the defense of Paul during one of his trials (Acts 23:9–10). Brief but positive events nonetheless.

Pharisees can trace their purpose to the beginning of the nation of Israel. God created the people of Israel and called them to live together in obedience according to his law. It was this very giving of the law and the command to the people to live in obedience to God through the law that both constituted the people of Israel and separated them from the pagan nations that surrounded them. As a result, Israel was very careful about association with other people lest their purity be tainted. They separated themselves from people who did not follow Torah (God's law), and entry into the community by one from the outside was conditioned upon the willingness to embrace Torah.*

It's easy to see how in this context a group would arise who felt it was their responsibility to hold the rest of the people to a high standard. This role *per se* is entirely proper. Jesus taught this (Luke 17:3). Paul's frequent admonition to us to encourage one another includes urging each other to hold onto and live by the tremendous truths of our faith. This is nothing new. This may be the ultimate answer to Cain's question, "Am I my brother's keeper?" (Gen. 4:9 NRSV). Yes, especially when it comes to encouraging a brother or sister to a deeper relationship with God.

The Pharisees accepted this role. They "did not think the religious hierarchy was doing a very good job of leading the people in holiness, so they took the trappings of priestly life upon themselves, though they were not priests."[2] The "Pharisees saw themselves as preserving covenant relationship to God by practicing holiness. . . . In

---

*From the Hebrew word meaning instruction, teaching, or law. It has a range of meanings, but most specifically means the first five books (Pentateuch) of the Bible.

their view, the best way to keep covenant relationship . . . with God was to keep holy by separating themselves from all that was unclean."[3] Rules to accomplish this multiplied exponentially. When Jesus began his public ministry, the Pharisees began to inspect his faithfulness to the law. Since Jesus "has repeatedly interpreted the law in ways that depart from conventions shared by the Pharisees, they are often cast as his antagonists."[4] Indeed, the friction between Jesus and the Pharisees must have been intense considering Jesus' habit of eating with sinners and inviting them into the kingdom, actions in sharp contrast to the pharisaical idea of separation from those things or people they judged as unholy. Let's be clear, the issue is not whether or not to live according to God's law, but how to do so. Jesus posed for everyone the question of what it means to live according to Torah. "How should those who love Torah act when they confront persons who go their own way, are unconcerned about the good of others, and are indifferent to what their actions mean for the future of their community?"[5] We hear today the question of how to live a life of respect for both God's holiness and his love for his creation.

So, were the Pharisees merely a bunch of hypocrites? No. We can see the importance to the nation of Israel of purity and obedience to God, which was the motive behind their practices. Larry Osborne writes,

> They were zealous for God, completely committed to their faith. They were theologically astute, masters of the biblical texts. They fastidiously obeyed even the most obscure commands. They even made up extra rules just in case they

> were missing anything. Their embrace of spiritual disciplines was second to none.[6]

Today we might look back on the many laws and attitudes toward keeping those laws as unduly harsh, but we have to remember that the very survival of Israel as a nation of God's people was at stake.

Still, though well aware of the importance of the purity of Israel, Jesus saw something in the general character and practice of the Pharisees to which he strongly objected. During his ministry, Jesus' encounters with the Pharisees were frequent and almost always negative. He was vocal in his criticism of them as a group; it might be said that he pulled no punches. Calling them sons of vipers is quite scathing in any context (Matt. 23:33). The Pharisees followed their religious practices in such a way that it caused them to reject Jesus and his teachings. We see the power of pharisaical attitudes when we realize the Pharisees allowed this to justify their involvement in Jesus' crucifixion.

Through these encounters with the Pharisees, we are offered an extremely important lesson. Luke reports a parable told by Jesus that is especially on point. It's the parable of the Pharisee and the tax collector. Luke 18 begins with Jesus teaching his disciples about prayer, then he seems to expand the audience beyond just the disciples to include anyone whose righteousness was focused on themselves.

> Then Jesus told this story to some who had great confidence in their own righteousness and scorned everyone else: "Two men went to the

> Temple to pray. One was a Pharisee, and the other was a despised tax collector. The Pharisee stood by himself and prayed this prayer: 'I thank you, God, that I am not like other people—cheaters, sinners, adulterers. I'm certainly not like that tax collector! I fast twice a week, and I give you a tenth of my income.'
>
> "But the tax collector stood at a distance and dared not even lift his eyes to heaven as he prayed. Instead, he beat his chest in sorrow, saying, 'O God, be merciful to me, for I am a sinner.' I tell you, this sinner, not the Pharisee, returned home justified before God. For those who exalt themselves will be humbled, and those who humble themselves will be exalted." (Luke 18:9–14)

This was a shocking reversal from the expectations of those listening. Jesus uses two caricatures to represent two extreme ways of responding to God. One is that of a Pharisee who the audience would immediately recognize as representing the very religious in Jewish culture. The other is that of a tax collector who would also be quickly recognized, but as one representing the very sinful in the culture. Following custom, both men went to the temple to pray as prayer was thought to be especially effective if offered in the temple. It was also customary to pray aloud. The Pharisee it seems assumed a position of honor where he "stood by himself," separated from others, too holy for them. His dress alone would announce that he was a Pharisee, and his actions only added to that identity. He began his prayer by calling out people from whom he was different, a list of sinners that included disdainfully "that tax collector." The Pharisee informed God and others how good he was, fasting twice a week and tithing. Indeed, the actions attributed to him exceed those required by the law. There was only one absolute day of fasting and that was on the Day of Atonement, though perhaps fasting on the Sabbath had become common. By emphasizing his faithfulness in tithing, the Pharisee drew a vivid contrast with a tax collector, who would be assumed to have cheated people out of their money, including that which could be used to pay the temple tax. It's clear, isn't it, who is at the center of his prayer? It's himself. The Pharisee stood in the presence of God and gave testimony to how good and how holy he was, with no thought that he could be a sinner. Note that he asks nothing of God, suggesting that in his own mind he needed nothing from God.[7] In his self-assessment he had arrived. The process was complete. In his view of his holiness he was self-sufficient and self-righteous.

The tax collector's actions and demeanor were quite different. As his means of employment put him on the margins of society, so it also would have removed him to the margins of the temple "at a distance." Those hearing Jesus tell this parable may have even been surprised at the thought of a tax collector in the temple at all. Praying in the temple probably would have made any tax collector feel ill at ease, evidenced in this parable by the fact that he would not even look up to offer his prayer to God. But he came to the temple in humility to meet with God. He beat his chest in sorrow and uttered a short, simple prayer, "Oh God, be merciful to me, for I am a sinner." The use of the definite article in the original text suggests that the tax collector is saying that he is *the* sinner, reminiscent of Paul's declaration that he was the worst of all sinners.[8]

At this point it might be helpful to have before us two concepts of holiness. One understanding, prominent in the Old Testament, views holiness as physical separation or consecration to God. We find this in application to things like Israel being a holy nation (Exod. 19:6), a holy place (Exod. 3:5), holy things such as the utensils used in the temple (Exod. 28:2), and holy people (Lev. 21:6; 1 Cor. 1:2). To be holy in this sense is to be dedicated to God and separated from all things unholy. When something holy comes in contact with something unholy, it too becomes unholy. The second understanding is about a transformation of one's heart, and the development of a new character as the image of Christ is formed in us. While there is a hint of the second understanding in the Old Testament as when God speaks of replacing a stony, stubborn heart with a tender, responsive one (Ezek. 11:19), the second understanding of holiness is primarily developed as a teaching of Jesus in the New Testament. Holiness is no longer purely ceremonial or external, but rather is seen essentially as conformity of the heart to the very nature of God. That nature is one of self-giving love. Jesus' conflict with the Pharisees was over what it meant to be holy. For the Pharisees, holy meant separation. Jesus lived and taught holiness as merciful and compassionate to others (Luke 6:36). We see Jesus in joyful fellowship with tax collectors, prostitutes, and other sinners without ever compromising on his own holiness.

The mistake of the Pharisees was their religious practice that caused them to elevate the outward conduct of keeping the law over the compassion of a transformed heart. It was not unlike Martha's elevation of doing over Mary's being (Luke 10:38–42). The Sabbath became more important than mercy (Matt. 12:1–13; John 9:13–17) and tradition more important than the commands of God (Matt. 15:1–3). Michael Mangis relates this flaw of the Pharisees to sloth, specifically spiritual sloth: "It is easier to check off a list of behaviors than to look into one's heart and sweep out the corners."[9] The Pharisees were judgmental, seeing sin in others but not in themselves (Matt. 9:10–11; Luke 7:36–39; John 8:3–5). The Pharisee in Jesus' parable based his righteousness on what he felt he had achieved and his self-righteousness. Then he used his opinion of his own holiness as justification to look down on others, even despising them. He missed the point that holiness comes only by the grace of God, and when that is the source it will bring unity among God's children not separation. It brings a spirit that is loving, gracious, gentle, and forgiving. It's not that we don't discern the presence or absence of spiritual growth in others. It's what we do with that discernment. Oswald Chambers writes, "When we discern that other people are not growing spiritually and allow that discernment to turn to criticism, we block our fellowship with God. God never gives us discernment so that we may criticize, but that we may intercede."[10]

The Pharisee of the parable missed the application of the Great Commandment to love God *and* love others, or as it has been paraphrased, love God for the sake of others. These commands were presented as inseparable by Jesus. "God cannot look upon a person as just, as long as he despises his neighbour."[11] The tax collector, on the other hand, must have been struck by his lack of holiness beside the holiness of God. He recognized his unworthiness, his sinfulness, and his need for God. "When we set our lives beside the life of Jesus and beside the holiness of God, all that is left to say is, 'God be merciful to me—the sinner.'"[12]

The restoration of the image of God is a transformation of the heart, which manifests in external behavior (Matt. 23:26). This teaching may also be found in the Sermon on the Mount. Jesus concludes this teaching by saying that when the attitudes expressed in these verses exist in a person, *he or she is then acting as a true child of the Father in heaven* (Matt. 5:45). He summarized these teachings in his final, incredible instruction, "But you are to be perfect, even as your Father in heaven is perfect" (Matt. 5:48). God created the human heart in his own image so that the human heart might reflect the divine heart. How amazing that Jesus' admonition that we are to be compassionate (merciful) in Luke 6:36 uses the Father's character as the model for this behavior. A person who approaches life and its relationships with a heart being formed in this manner does so in a radically different way.

The mistake of the Pharisees is neither rare nor limited in scope. It is a tendency that has plagued religious people in every age. Our purpose here is not to simply criticize or analyze the Pharisees, but to be able to recognize and avoid (or eliminate) these mistakes in our lives. The failings of the Pharisees may easily be the failings of anyone following disciplines of spiritual formation. So, how do we avoid the mistake of the Pharisees? Larry Osborne writes, "We can't earn our way into God's favor by meticulously following a moral code—even a biblical one. Our deeds will never be righteous enough. God's standard of holiness is way beyond our best efforts."[13] That would seem to present a problem. If we can't earn or develop our own holiness, where does that leave us?

Spiritual formation rooted in self-reference or self-help such as that of the Pharisees is actually rooted in the fallen nature which itself needs to be transformed. Care must be taken to avoid self-reference, even when the focus of the reform is on internal change. Christians can become so wrapped up in how to become better Christians that this becomes the end rather than the means:

> Their concern seems mostly to center around self, although they hope that their spiritual growth will automatically osmose into those around them. . . . *But the goal of authentic spirituality is a life which escapes from the closed circle of spiritual self-indulgence, or even self-improvement, to become absorbed in the love of God and other persons.* For the essence of spiritual renewal is "the love of God . . . poured out within our hearts through the Holy Spirit" (Rom. 5:5 NASB). . . . Religious forms of self-improvement can also generate nervous self-concern and spiritual pride. If growth is built on repressed guilt, or if the means of growth is a set of laws to be followed or an intricate and arduous path to be mastered, spiritual self-centeredness will result.[14]

When believers are brought to this deeper level of righteousness of which Jesus speaks (Matt. 5:20), they can stop emphasizing lists of activities as of *first importance* and start thinking about who they are on a deeper level in Christ. We can begin to pray that the love of God be poured into and through our heart. The focus becomes more and more our identity and nature growing out of intimacy with God. The external life will then follow the heart.

The goal is to become absorbed in the love of God and other persons. Sure, we are to practice all of the spiritual disciplines—prayer, fasting, study of the Word, etc. (doing)—but we understand these are means of grace that lead us into an ever-deepening relationship of love with God and others (being). We find this process in Jesus' words about the true vine in John 15, "Those who abide in me and I in them bear much fruit . . ." (v. 5 NRSV). I especially like this use of *abide* found in many translations. Think of the verbs Jesus could have chosen: *persevere, persist, endure, develop, survive,* and more. Instead of verbs that might emphasize our actions, he used a verb that emphasizes relationship and trust in him.

Rather than being found in external ritual, denial of self (required in order to be absorbed in the love of God and others) goes to the very core of one's being, the place where the Holy Spirit meets and transforms believers. This is where a change of heart occurs. "It is not a question of giving up sin, but of giving up my right to myself, my natural independence, and my self-will. This is where the battle has to be fought."[15] Any believer can engage in a self-referenced effort to change, but what is called for is a radical, loving abandonment to God (the first commandment) for the sake of others (the second like it).

Let's take this one step further. To follow Jesus is to be called to live in courageous faith. It is appropriately applied here. We are invited to ask, "What is the character of the courageous faith that is required to grow in a life of holiness lived as Jesus lived?" Jesus chose humility as the frame for his answer. Humility is a powerful position in life when it means allowing our inexhaustible Father to be the source and sufficiency of our life. This requires us to have the courageous faith to surrender our right to our self, our natural independence, and our self-will. In avoiding the mistake of the Pharisees, we are called to an abiding in Jesus that allows the love of God to be poured out through us. It goes against that natural, fallen self within us and it's not likely to be appreciated by the world in which we live, but this faith or trust in God is the very core of the spiritual life. Growing in our ability to live in holiness as Jesus lived is a journey we are on together, encouraging each other while remembering the unfailing love our Father in heaven has for us.

Reflection and Application

1. One of the disciplines of spiritual formation is learning to express ourselves well on our biblical beliefs. It requires time and effort and is usually a real struggle. However, a time will come when God will use this in the life of another person. If we satisfy ourselves with using someone else's words, those words will never be fully effective. We should make it a practice to thoroughly think through our beliefs. A great place to start this is to state in your own words the meaning of

holiness. Where is the call to holiness challenging you and how will you respond?

2. In Genesis 2, we read the startling but marvelous revelation that God created humanity in his image. From this we understand that spiritual formation is one's transformation into the image of God through the work of the Holy Spirit. In the New Testament this takes on the understanding of becoming like Jesus since Jesus is the fullness of God, i.e., the image of God. But the Pharisees were missing something. From what you know about them, if the Pharisees were around today what characteristics would they attribute to a person they consider to be in the image of God? What might be missing?

3. This is not a condemnation of healthy habits of practicing the means of grace. Let's be sure we understand the differences between devotional habits and the works of the Pharisees. Reflect on your habits. Ask the Holy Spirit to show you ways to avoid ritual and increasingly make your habits a matter of the heart.

4. In the tax collector's short prayer, what expressions of faith/trust in God may be found?

5. What is one thought you can take from this chapter to reflect upon in the days ahead with the guidance of the Holy Spirit? What is one prayer over which you will spend time with the Lord?

3

Dry Seasons

We must find our contentment in the execution of His will, whether He leads us by sufferings or by consolations, so that everything should seem the same to a person who has truly abandoned himself. We must remain faithful in the dry periods by which God proves our love for Him.

—Brother Lawrence

I wonder if you or someone you know has had this experience. You have trusted God for your salvation and know Jesus as your Savior. You have embraced spiritual disciplines such as prayer, study of the Bible, worship, and fellowship as regular commitments. You know what it is to grow in your relationship with your Father in heaven and expect greater warmth and deeper intimacy in that relationship. But instead, it has come to feel cool and distant. Prayers seem to be ineffective. Perhaps doubts have begun to creep in regarding some promises and rather than bringing hope they now seem hollow. Then there are worse thoughts. Have you done something to offend God? Why has God withdrawn his favor from you? If the sense of distance and abandonment deepens, you may even ask if God singled you out for some unfair reason to be treated like this. *Where are you, God?* At their very worst, these thoughts can threaten faith to its core.

In the hymn "O for a Closer Walk with God" the poet and hymnodist William Cowper wrote, "Where is the blessedness I knew when first I saw the Lord? Where is the soul refreshing view of Jesus and his word?" These haunting words trouble the hearts of most believers. These are the thoughts and feelings of a dry season, a time when it doesn't seem as if God is responding to us or is present to us. This experience is not unique to our relationship with God. It can be experienced in many relationships. The closer the relationship, the greater the expectations. The greater the expectations for the relationship, the greater the potential of a dry season, and the greater the possible consequences.

The Psalms set the emotional extremes before us. We often hear the strength and joy of relationship. "The Lord is my strength and shield. I trust him with all my heart. He helps me, and my heart is filled with joy. I burst out in songs of thanksgiving" (Ps. 28:7). "Taste and see that the Lord is good. Oh, the joys of those who take refuge in him! (Ps. 34:8). "I long, yes, I faint with longing to enter the courts of the Lord. With my whole being, body and soul, I will shout joyfully to the living God" (Ps. 84:2).

But with the marvelous integrity we find in the Bible, we also hear the anguished laments. "O Lord, how long will you forget me? Forever? How long will you look the other way?" (Ps. 13:1). "O Lord, come back to us! How long will you delay? Take pity on your servants!" (Ps. 90:13). Both praise and lament have a place in a life of faith, keeping us in touch with both confidence in God and the full realities of life. Dry seasons are common in many contexts, but unlike those in human relationships, we need to remember that God, in sovereign love, can use dry seasons for our good to mold a stronger relationship and character. This beckons us to a deeper understanding of this lonely, often confusing time. How do we view dry seasons in a proper light? What does courageous faith require of us in times like these?

In spiritual formation, two things should be remembered regarding dry seasons. First, one seriously seeking God will almost certainly experience them. The Psalms, Job, Lamentations, and Habakkuk all contain laments and confirm that the life of faith is not for the weak of heart or for those who insist on a life of ease. Even the spiritual giants of the Christian faith have experienced dry seasons and have spoken about the challenges that come with them. We should not be surprised, then, if we encounter dry seasons ourselves. But still we ask, "What is going on?" It should not be lost on us how incredible it is that we have a heavenly Father who allows us to voice these questions. Also worthy of note, it is only when we are in a significant, meaningful relationship with God that we can notice a change in that relationship. It is only when we desire a close, growing relationship with God that we can feel what seems to be a cooling. Without relationship there would be no dry seasons.

The second point to remember is that the response to dry seasons is perseverance while trusting for the blessing in their midst. Oswald Chambers reminds us, "If you are going through a time of discouragement, there is a time of great personal growth ahead."[1] Yet, it is not uncommon for someone experiencing a dry season to give up on spiritual disciplines such as prayer, solitude, and reading of the Word. While this might seem a reasonable response to something that seems so unproductive, it is precisely the opposite of the perseverance expected by the Lord. If indeed as the Lord promises he will use dry seasons, to abandon spiritual disciplines in such times assures that any lesson the Lord is teaching will be missed.

The life of Jeremiah offers to lead us to a deeper understanding of what it means to have courageous faith during dry seasons. Jeremiah was born near Jerusalem, the son of a priest. He was called to be a prophet at an early age in the days of the decline of the Assyrian Empire under whose yoke Judah had existed for many years. His career spanned the reign of five kings of Judah. The decline of the Assyrian Empire and the recommitment of the people to God under King Josiah brought a time of hope for the future of the nation, but it was a hope that was to be short-lived. It seems that from early in his ministry, Jeremiah was convinced of a dire fate for his people. When faced with the rise of the Babylonian Empire, some of Judah's leaders and false prophets proclaimed the certain survival of Judah as a nation based on the presence of Solomon's temple in Jerusalem. They reasoned that the presence of Solomon's temple was proof of God's favor and nothing bad would be allowed to happen to them. Jeremiah, on the other hand, foresaw the capture of Judah, the destruction of Jerusalem, and the exile of its people to Babylon.

Jeremiah was called by God to be a prophet for this time, to call the people of Judah to trust God for their survival, not the symbolism of Solomon's temple. In place of false hope, Jeremiah insisted that "authentic hope must bear the scars of disaster and embrace the harsh realities of the shattered world."[2] In other words, authentic hope is not separated from the vicissitudes of life. It prevails through the good and the bad. Good points to always remember, but Jeremiah's message was unwelcome and was received with agitation and resentment. When his prophecies did not immediately come true, people laughed at him and mocked him. They made fun of his warnings, persecuted him, and attempted to kill him. Even his family hoped for his downfall. But God had said, "I am with you to deliver you" (1:8). Based on the promises God had made to him, Jeremiah expected to be vindicated by divine justice on the wrongdoers. Instead, just the opposite seemed to be happening. Jeremiah felt abandoned, forsaken by the very one who called him. In this perceived abandonment, it was not that God was not speaking, but he was perceived as not helping as expected, not protecting, not keeping his promise. Jeremiah believed he had been forgotten by God, thus his plea, "remember me and visit me" (Jer. 15:15 NSRV).

Jeremiah's complaint was that he had been a willing, joyful, and faithful servant of God, but what had his service gotten him? His confidence in God was shaken and his faith was hanging by a thread. Humiliated, Jeremiah wanted to quit, but could not; he cursed the day of his birth, but went on living. And in his weaknesses we also see strengths. Ostracized, excluded from the simplest joys of companionship, totally isolated, Jeremiah expressed his lament: "Why then does my suffering continue? Why is my wound so incurable? Your help seems as uncertain as a seasonal brook, like a spring that has gone dry" (Jer. 15:18). I want to say, "Wait a minute! This is Jeremiah saying this? This is one of the greatest, most courageous prophets of the Lord uttering these words?" In Jeremiah's time, there were few things more important than a reliable source of water. This source had to be dependable. We can envision a weary traveler coming to a life-sustaining brook, or a shepherd guiding his thirsty flock to an oft-visited spring. How distressing, even life-threatening, if the source of water is found to have failed. But this is exactly what Jeremiah was expressing as what he felt was coming from the relationship in that moment.

Jeremiah's lament was spiritual candor, and God was not shocked or outraged. In it we see and are comforted by a very human prophet, one plagued by a sense of inadequacy, moods of depression, doubt, and despair. But even in making the complaint, we find evidence of hope. Despite his anguish, Jeremiah still turned to God, remaining faithful to his call, and is a model for an honest relationship with God. Underneath his frustration and confusion, Jeremiah was a man of courageous faith, confidence, and, above all, prayer. This is highlighted dramatically when, in one of his depressed moments, he was nevertheless able to say, "O Lord, if you heal me, I will be truly healed; if you save me, I will be truly saved. My praises are for you alone!" (17:14).

Indeed, God was faithful to Jeremiah and to his people, but his faithfulness came in ways not expected. He did not bring an end to persecution and reproach, but the promise of strength to endure so that they could continue in God's service despite the certain conflict that would be experienced for God's sake. God, who is our only comfort, calls us to serve and, if necessary, to bear reproach for his sake.

Job also experienced suffering, such that he desired to confront God face-to-face and to prove the injustice of his suffering. But Job's faith still allowed him to say, "God might kill me, but I have no other hope" (Job 13:15). Such faith is precious to the Lord. There was a point in Jesus' ministry when difficult teaching caused many of his disciples to turn away and desert him. Jesus turned to the Twelve and asked, "'Are you also going to leave?' Simon Peter replied, 'Lord, to whom would we go? You have the words that give eternal life'" (John 6:67–68). And, of course, we remember the ultimate example of faithful service of Jesus in the garden of Gethsemane, "My Father! If it is possible, let this cup of suffering be taken away from me. Yet I want your will to be done, not mine" (Matt. 26:39).

Thomas à Kempis knew that love and praise for Jesus comes easily when comfort, consolation, and support are being received from him. But when Jesus seems to hide himself and leave the believer for even a brief period, the attitude can turn into complaining and depression. He imagines a conversation between Jesus and one of his followers:

> Don't think that you are totally abandoned if for a time I have sent you some trial or have withdrawn the consolation you sought, for this is the road that leads you to the kingdom of heaven. Doubtless, it is better for you, and for my other

> servants too, to undergo these trials than to have everything come out just as you desired.[3]

This would certainly not be our first, natural, human choice, to go through trials rather than have everything come out as we desire. In his *Introduction to the Devout Life*, Francis de Sales writes to an inquirer named Philothea with advice for spiritual formation, touching on the perspective one should maintain when seeking God in the dry seasons:

> If it should happen that you find no joy or comfort in meditation, Philothea, I urge you not to be disturbed but to open your heart's door to words of vocal prayer. . . . After this if you have not received any consolation do not be disturbed, no matter how great the dryness may be, but continue to keep a devout posture before God. How many courtiers go a hundred times a year into the prince's audience chamber without any hope of speaking to him but merely to be seen by him and do their duty. We too, my dear Philothea, ought to approach holy prayer purely and simply to do our duty and testify to our fidelity.[4]

Brother Lawrence was born Nicholas Herman in eastern France. After an injury sustained in the Thirty Years War forced him out of the army, he entered a Discalced Carmelite monastery where he remained for the rest of his life. Considering that his primary assignments were working in the kitchen and repairing sandals, we might not naturally look to him for spiritual insights that would benefit others for centuries. But in the midst of these seemingly trivial tasks, Brother Lawrence made the practice of the awareness of the presence of God in all things and at all times the focus of his life. Yet, even he had words of advice to share about those times when God does not seem to be present:

> We must find our contentment in the execution of His will, whether He leads us by sufferings or by consolations, so that everything should seem the same to a person who has truly abandoned himself. We must remain faithful in the dry periods by which God proves our love for Him.[5]

God proves our love for him. That's an interesting twist on what we would usually say. We may from time to time be bold enough to say we want to prove our love for God, which usually means in our way and in our time. How often do we want God to prove his love for us? Again and again through gifts of health, wealth, and other blessings. Brother Lawrence sees a season in which God proves or refines our love for him. What does this mean? It means dry seasons may be times when our faith in God grows deeper, a time when we may learn to love God for who he is, not for the things he does for us. Isn't this what we hear in traditional wedding vows? For better or worse, for richer or poorer, in sickness and in health. In other words, to love and cherish without condition. Dry periods remind us that God is to be followed because God is God, not because of any benefits we may expect from following him. That, indeed, is a deeper lesson in spiritual maturity.

There is a place for candor in our conversations with God. Some people feel uneasy with the thought of any expression of discontent with God, much less anger. "Anger at God often goes unacknowledged or unexpressed. Why are many Christians unable to either acknowledge or express their anger at God? Because many learn from family, church and subcultures that being angry with God is wrong."[6] A submissive/passive view instructs that we should accept what comes as caused or allowed by God, and that to question or complain, as Jeremiah and Job did, would be a lack of faith. We certainly want to be cautious on this point. Disrespect or dishonor of God is not acceptable, but lament is not unbelief and need not be disrespectful. We are permitted to question why and to have the emotions that appropriately accompany that question. Furthermore, a false pretense of unwavering piety carries with it the danger of making it harder for others who are struggling with feelings of abandonment, adding guilt rather than encouragement to their struggle.

Unresolved anger in any relationship creates silence, emotional withdrawal, feelings of distance and disconnection, even alienation. God understands our humanity and invites resolution of our questions. The Psalms extend the invitation to "Pour out your heart to him" (Ps. 62:8). This is an invitation to tell God everything going on within us, including our emotions. After all, God knows our innermost thoughts whether we express them or not. "The laments of Jeremiah, the psalmists, and others who continue to hold fast to God are a reminder that the God who loves us does not desert when summer fades but, when the difficult days arrive, keeps a ready ear open to our cries."[7] When a mother hugs a child with a skinned knee, the knee doesn't immediately heal, but the hug is comforting nonetheless. The sense that we are heard by God and accepted as children has the potential to be incredibly powerful for building and restoring that relationship; for letting us know and experience the deep warmth that is true to our relationship with God.

We could view dry seasons as a particular form of suffering. As many spiritual teachers have discovered, dry seasons are difficult times, especially because of the sense of abandonment that accompanies them. The divine promises that God is present, that he is sovereign, and that he loves his children with holy love allow the believer to press through these times. Perhaps the Lord intended to deepen one's prayer life, leading to prayers on God's terms rather than the predetermined expectations of the believer. If the discipline of the dry season is abandoned, such lessons and the joy of seeing how God responds through such times would be missed. After this life, there will never again be dry seasons from which the child of God may learn.

God's ways can be difficult to understand, even beyond present understanding. In the writings of Isaiah is found the reminder that "just as the heavens are higher than the earth, so [God's] ways are higher than your ways and [God's] thoughts higher than your thoughts" (Isa. 55:9). This is a call to trust at its deepest level. Trust by its very nature must be put into action. Without this, trust may be present in word but it is not present as a reality that has been annealed by fire. If the desire of God for the spiritual life of the believer is a deeper and deeper level of trust, this can only be accomplished through a deeper and deeper level of growth. Only God, in his wisdom, knows what will strengthen and mature the trust of a follower of Jesus.

What is the substance of courageous faith in the encounter of dry seasons? How is it cultivated? True, the life of faith is not for the fainthearted. It's not a life of ease and worldly privilege. Yet we are called to live it with the determination of an athlete pressing toward victory. Our ability to live in the reality of Jesus is dependent on the indwelling Holy Spirit. The Holy Spirit may work in mysterious ways, but most often I believe he works through our spiritual disciplines. For dry seasons, the discipline of remembering is especially important. It's a discipline seen throughout the Bible. Joshua invoked this discipline when, following the Lord's instruction, he set up stones in the Jordan River as a memorial to what the Lord did when Israel crossed into the promised land. Near the end of his life in his final words to Israel, Joshua called on the people to remember what the Lord had already done. The Lord brought Abraham from a distant land and led him to the land of Canaan; he gave Abraham many descendants; he sent Moses and Aaron to Egypt and brought the Hebrew slaves out as free people; he sustained the people in the wilderness for forty years; he drove out the inhabitants of the land promised to Israel. As a preface to his charge to the people in his final words to them, Joshua tells them to remember!

Many of these events were still being commemorated in the days of Jesus. Passover and the Festival of Unleavened Bread related to the delivery of the people from Egypt. The Feast of Tabernacles celebrates God's provision and protection for the people of Israel during their forty years of wandering in the wilderness. The Day of Atonement commemorates the annual sacrifice by the High Priest for the sins of the people. All of these call the people to remember the faithfulness of God in their lives.

The greatest memorial was instituted by Jesus himself. As he celebrated the Passover meal with his disciples, Jesus broke the bread and gave it to them saying, "This is my body, which is given for you. Do this in remembrance of me." After supper he took the cup saying, "This cup is the new covenant between God and his people—an agreement confirmed with my blood. Do this in remembrance of me as often as you drink it" (1 Cor. 11:23–25). In our lives as disciples, we are told to remember God's faithfulness, and Jesus is telling us how important it is that we regularly, continuously remember him.

The question is, can we face dry seasons in the light of the faithfulness of God or will they hinder and harm our faith? In other words, can we persevere in dry seasons, whether short or long, anchored in what has been revealed to us in the life, death, and resurrection of Jesus? Throughout Scripture there is one adjective that accompanies God's love more than any other: steadfast. Pray, listen, praise, worship, read, and reflect on the steadfast love of God. We are created in the image of God, but we must be molded into that image. Courageous faith allows God to use dry seasons to mold us in his image, to mold our character into the likeness of his character. Courageous faith has moved beyond expecting God to prove his goodness over and over again and instead allows God to prove our love for him.

Reflection and Application

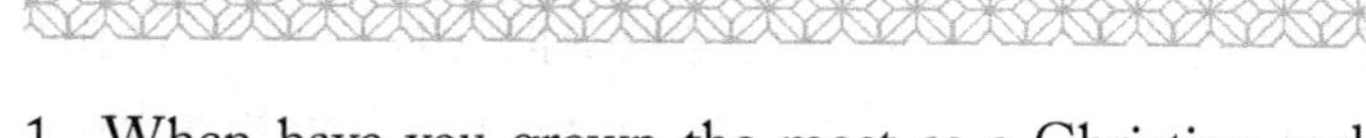

1. When have you grown the most as a Christian and why? What experience have you had or are you aware of regarding dry seasons? How might there be a unique opportunity for spiritual growth in a dry season?

2. Brother Lawrence is known for his efforts to develop intimacy with God through awareness of God's presence in every activity of the day. He makes the counterintuitive statement that God proves our love for him in the dry seasons. What does this statement mean to you? How do you think this happens?

3. Did Jesus ever experience a dry season? Who are others in the Bible that you think of as having gone through a season in which the Lord seemed distant?

4. Suppose someone comes to you for advice. They are a follower of Jesus who understands the importance of spiritual discipline. But they are experiencing a period of dryness. From the information and experiences mentioned in this chapter and your own experience, what advice would you give to them? How else might you help them?

5. What is one thought you can take from this chapter to reflect upon in the days ahead with the guidance of the Holy Spirit? What is one prayer over which you will spend time with the Lord?

4

The Problem of Suffering

Even though the fig trees have no blossoms, and there are no grapes on the vines; even though the olive crop fails, and the fields lie empty and barren; even though the flocks die in the fields, and the cattle barns are empty, yet I will rejoice in the Lord*! I will be joyful in the God of my salvation! The Sovereign* Lord *is my strength! He makes me as surefooted as a deer, able to tread upon the heights.*

—Habakkuk 3:17–19

We need to be honest about the problem of suffering. It's not a simple problem for which there are simple answers. Simple answers can do more harm than good. It's complex, and we have sought to understand it since the beginning of time. It has been said that God has in the cross and resurrection of Christ overcome, and indeed he has, but that victory is not yet fully manifest. We do not yet have in our present experience that victory of God which wipes away all tears. Even the best and most innocent of people still have trials and tribulations, and all still die. The honest answer is that after centuries of seeking, we are not likely to get particular answers that bring an end to our asking why this is the case.[1] The religious thought of

Jesus' time tried to make it simple, hence when the disciples saw a blind man they asked, "Why was this man born blind? Was it because of his own sin or his parents' sins?" Jesus rejected the simple answer and instead pointed to the blindness as a way for the power of God to be shown (John 9:1–4). Even in his own suffering on the cross, Jesus does not provide a simple answer for us. Quoting from Psalm 22, Jesus said, "My God, my God, why have you abandoned me?" (Matt. 27:46). Yet even in this time of desolation, Jesus expresses his trust. "Father, I entrust my spirit into your hands!" (Luke 23:46). There seems to have been room in his humanity for Jesus to express grief as to why within the sovereignty of God there was such suffering. In this way he is not separate from us but like us in the question over which we agonize. Jesus is our ultimate model, and whatever the circumstance, Jesus was steadfast in his trust in the faithful goodness of his Father. Perhaps one thing we understand from Jesus' words is that it is okay to ask why.

So we ask why, with the goal of learning more about courageous faith in the face of suffering. A common response to suffering is, "If indeed God is good and all powerful, he would not let this happen!" Suffering, whether we experience it ourselves or observe it, can raise questions about how God's love can coexist with suffering. It has the potential to greatly impact our understanding of God and our relationship with him. Thus, suffering must be addressed in any serious pursuit of spiritual formation. How do we keep tribulation from hindering our faith? Even more, how do we respond to suffering in a way that grows our faith?

Deep faith in the goodness of God is not an answer that brings a sigh of relief. It's an answer that points to overcoming but not to eliminating suffering. Faith is easy to propose in the face of suffering but will never be adequate as a mere platitude. True faith is a faith that is formed and sustained in the context of doubts and anger that seem to be the rational, natural response to suffering. As failure of trust in God is evident in the fall of humankind, the return to a dependent trust in God is at the very heart of spiritual maturity. Suffering and the questions and doubts raised by suffering present for many today the greatest challenge to a deep trust in God. We are left with the paradox that somehow suffering has a place within the power of our loving God. We live within this paradox, called to trust God regardless of the circumstances over which God has control.

The Bible promises that God can and does use sorrow and suffering, trials and tribulation. The Old Testament prophets speak of God using hardship and even disaster to turn Israel back to faith. For Israel, the oppression that came from its enemies must have raised fears that God had abandoned his chosen people. On the contrary, the biblical perspective which looks back over time actually shows the loving care of God. Like a fond and loving father, he was trying to wean them away from trust in kings or princes or in armies or the powers of this world. He was trying to teach them, again and again, that their faith must be in him alone. He was leading them, through every trial and in every age, to the realization that God alone is faithful in all tribulations, that he alone is constant in his love and must be clung to, even when it seems all else has been turned upside down.[2]

The lessons for Israel as a nation are also lessons to be learned by individuals. One of the best-known Bible verses assures believers that "God causes everything to work together for the good of those who love God and are called according to his purpose for them" (Rom. 8:28). Many throughout the history of the church have shared their rich experience in coming to understand this promise and overcoming the spiritual defeat threatened by suffering. Thomas à Kempis writes, "He who knows how to suffer enjoys the greatest peace, and such a man is victor over himself, master of the world, friend of Christ, and heir of heaven."[3] This is very different from a stoic acceptance of suffering or a stiff upper lip. The believer is challenged to move to a deeper understanding of suffering that is firmly and essentially rooted in trust of God.

As all suffering is not from the same cause, neither will the way God uses suffering always be for the same purpose. Some will suffer because of their allegiance to Jesus. Others may suffer precisely because they are bearing the suffering of others. Some will suffer simply because they are in a world where suffering is a reality, a world known as "fallen Babylon" (Rev. 18:2). It is not unusual that the greatest saints, those who have made the greatest contribution to the kingdom on earth, are those who have suffered the most. History is filled with stories of Christians who were willing to stand up for their faith, from early church martyrs such as Stephen to many believers today where the church is under severe persecution. The list of those persecuted for their faith in Jesus is tragically long. The church in Korea suffered intense persecution during the Japanese occupation from 1910–1945. The intent of the persecution was to destroy the church, and many pastors made the ultimate sacrifice during those years. The result, though, was that it drove the church to prayer, and the church became one of the greatest praying churches in history and experienced a season of remarkable growth. Suffering such as experienced by the church in Korea represents that which will come in some fashion, and to some degree, to many Christians. It is a tragedy that continues in numerous parts of the world today, but when this suffering is embraced from a proper perspective, God uses it for good.

Paul was allowed to experience suffering in order to remain humble. Suffering was an antidote to pride. Understandably, Paul's desire was that the thorn in the flesh be removed, and he prayed three times toward that end (2 Cor. 12:7). The answer that came was different from that for which he asked. "The answer came that the trial was a blessing; that, in the weakness and humiliation it brought, the grace and strength of the Lord could be better manifested."[4] Suffering became the means of reorientation from self to God. Importantly, though, the blessing is the use the Lord makes of suffering, rather than the suffering itself. "Suffering—hurt, difficulty and setbacks—establishes the context in which we either open our hearts and know the love of God or turn away in hardness, anger and self-pity."[5] Paul embraced suffering in a way that led him closer to God. "He welcomed heartbreak, disillusionment, and tribulation for only one reason—these things kept him unmovable in his devotion to the gospel of God."[6] Suffering strengthened Paul's resolve to proclaim the gospel. Perhaps the suffering caused him to see clearly that the hope offered by God is often the only answer for suffering.

The classic presentation of suffering is found in the book of Job. In the account of Job's life, it is said that he suffered because God allowed him to be afflicted by Satan. Satan's design was to show Job to be faithful only when everything was going well, not when his life fell apart. To Job, the suffering seemed beyond explanation. He could find no cause for it within himself and was urged to renounce his trust in God in the face of what seemed to be an irrational and undeserved condition of suffering. But Job did not curse God as his wife counseled. Rather, he tried in vain to demand an explanation from God. In the end, Job realized he could only stand in awe of almighty God in his immeasurable greatness. He came to a deeper acceptance of the sovereign power of God and that his ways are beyond humankind's ability to question. The truth is not always a satisfying answer, nevertheless it remains the truth.

While suffering may be brought on by one's own actions, the suffering that is the most difficult to understand is that which seems to be inflicted on the innocent. Peggy Reynoso writes of tragedy in her own family that brought this kind of suffering. Her nineteen-year-old daughter was killed in a terrible car accident. When Reynoso first saw the body in the casket, it was so shattered that she felt she had walked into the wrong chapel. But then, as she was able to bring the horror of the moment before the Lord, she heard an inaudible voice say, "I felt that way, too."[7]

This suffering, the worst a parent can endure, challenged Reynoso to an unswerving, unequivocal trust in God, a trust that endures irrational suffering. A response to such suffering, experienced by many, can only be found in faith that is contingent upon nothing, that flows directly from uncompromised confidence in the overarching goodness of God. It is a claim of hope rather than a surrender to hopelessness without God. Through this tragedy and its horrendous pain, Reynoso came to understand that God can use suffering for good, for refining the image of God in the believer, the image of the Father who allowed the Son to suffer for the sake of others.

Suffering can be profoundly transformative. "For the follower of Jesus, no suffering is without meaning in our formation in Christ."[8] Reynoso quotes Dietrich Bonhoeffer: "It is good to learn early enough that suffering and God is not a contradiction, but rather a necessary unity; for me the idea that God himself is suffering has always been one of the most convincing teachings of Christianity."[9] Bonhoeffer not only knew of Jesus' suffering on the cross, he also knew that the love of the Father which Jesus acknowledged in the high priestly prayer of John 17 was not suspended during the Passion. It remained fully in place, undiminished in any way through Jesus' arrest, trial, and crucifixion. It seems likely that this thought brought Bonhoeffer consolation when he himself was martyred.

Let's extend these ideas as far as we are able. Remember, the focus of God's discipline of those he loves is not time but eternity! To understand how suffering is being used and how trusting dependence upon God is always the appropriate response requires a perspective beyond the present moment of suffering. The perspective that brings clarity to suffering may be the entirety of one's life. Indeed, an eternal perspective may be the only lens through which suffering can be seen as overcome by the good, redeeming work of the sovereign God. Learning to trust in God's sovereignty is about more than just sticking it out through a time of suffering. It's about being able to call on that trust in other circumstances. When we can do that, we are more suitable to be used by God.

It has even been suggested that God uses suffering to prepare us in ways eternal. There are lessons of agape love, love that seeks the very best of another, that can only be learned through deep suffering. How could God be using suffering to prepare us for eternal life? "[God's] Bride-elect is in training for the throne. She is in the school of suffering to learn agape love to qualify her for rulership in an economy where the law of love is supreme."[10] There may be no better teacher than suffering to produce trust, and that same trust frees us to love our neighbor. The person who has made the most secular success but who reaches life's end without learning love has totally failed. Do not envy those in the limelight of publicity, those with scintillating intellects, or those who have accumulated great wealth and all that it affords. If one has not learned love in the process, his life is a disaster (Ps. 37).[11]

Suffering contains a unique ability to cause the disciple of Jesus to turn to God in faith (trust), because in a fallen world faith is the only true place left to turn. Suffering makes "[us] enter into our inner selves and acknowledge that we are in a place of exile and that we ought not to rely on anything in this world."[12] The suffering that is used by God can help the follower of Jesus to release false worldly dependencies and put his or her hope in God. Peter writes:

> These trials will show that your faith is genuine. It is being tested as fire tests and purifies gold—though your faith is far more precious than mere gold. So when your faith remains strong through many trials, it will bring you much praise and glory and honor on the day when Jesus Christ is revealed to the whole world. (1 Peter 1:7)

Remember these points about suffering as well. A proper understanding of suffering destroys any notion that God punishes his children as a form of vengeance. Suffering does not mean God has withdrawn his love any more than lack of suffering is proof of his love. "In fact, the time when it is most critical to discern and know the love of God is the time of suffering."[13] Furthermore, even when the benefits brought out of suffering by the hand of God are taken into account, suffering is not something to be sought. Suffering for the sake of suffering is not something God wants or originally intended.[14] Peter tells believers that there is a sense in which they are called to suffer and to follow in the steps of Jesus in suffering (1 Peter 2:21), but he refers to suffering that comes from obedience:

> This is not a masochistic seeking of suffering but a choice to accept the same cost of obedience that Jesus endured. We do not choose suffering, but as we try to live out the values of God's kingdom

> in a world that does not submit to Him, conflict and suffering inevitably result. This formational suffering is unique to the Christ follower.[15]

It would also be unrealistic and unsuitable to greet suffering with eagerness or feigned happiness. Living for God in the midst of suffering does not render sadness and grief inappropriate. While it seems paradoxical to embrace suffering, doing so as an act of trust in the goodness and sovereignty of God is precisely the means by which we affirm and deepen that trust and appropriate God's love as our own. The Bible presents many paradoxes for which it makes no excuse.

Take Habakkuk. The prophet cannot understand how God has allowed his country to get into the state it's in. The law has been mocked; evil is getting away with everything. He cries out to God, and God replies by saying that he's going to do something that even Habakkuk won't believe. Then the surprising revelation is that God intends to use a pagan nation to punish Israel. But in this story and prayer, Habakkuk's whole understanding of God is being reframed. At the end of the book, Habakkuk still doesn't have resolution. He doesn't understand why God is doing what he has proclaimed. Disaster is coming on Habakkuk's nation. But with a sense of conviction he affirms his trust beyond his circumstances. "Even though the fig trees have no blossoms, and there are no grapes on the vines; even though the olive crop fails, and the fields lie empty and barren; even though the flocks die in the fields, and the cattle barns are empty, yet I will rejoice in the LORD! I will be joyful in the God of my salvation!" (Hab. 3:17–18).

"That is the tension that we need to be able to define and discover. Not easy solutions, not a cop-out, but real, raw faith that confronts the difficulty of our world and Scripture, and is still able to confess trust in God."[16]

Suffering brings us face-to-face with the promise of God's presence and trust in his sovereign love. I would never compare my experience with suffering to anyone else's. Still, as I was writing this book, I went through a season of physical pain like nothing I had ever experienced. Over a few months, the pain was simply awful. Sleep came in brief, restless bouts. In the middle of one sleepless night, when no place or position or medicine would make the pain go away, I prayed, "Lord, I know you can take this pain away. I won't tell anyone if you don't want me to. It can just be our secret!" The pain didn't diminish, not even a little. I can't say I was surprised, or even disappointed. But the question came back, Is it even worth it to talk with the Lord about this? Then the thought came to me; while the tribulation had not been removed, I did have a strong sense of the Lord's presence with me in its midst. That's all the Lord promises. We can take this too lightly. Sometimes, and in this fallen world it seems all too often, that's what we have from God. If we are attentive and will receive it, we have the comfort of his presence and his loving reassurance that everything will be fine. We know his timing is not ours, but in his time everything will be fine.

The consistent biblical picture of God is that he does not shield us from sorrow and tribulation, but neither is he absent in our suffering. He promises, "When you go through deep waters, I will be with you. When you go through rivers of difficulty, you will not drown. When you walk through the fire of oppression, you will not be burned up; the flames will not consume you" (Isa. 43:2). Note carefully what God promises. With suffering comes an opportunity to form trust in the believer as nothing else can, and that trust becomes a powerful tool in God's hand. As Peggy Reynoso asked a friend, "How is it that the most dreadful things that happen to us are those that most increase our trust in God?"[17] Suffering is never sought nor regarded lightly, but suffering properly embraced matures trust. Trust matured today means greater trust for the future, both for the one enduring suffering and for those observing the victory of the disciple of Jesus.

Charles and Lettie Cowman were pioneer missionaries in Japan with the Oriental Missionary Society (now One Mission Society) at the turn of the twentieth century. Lettie wrote her classic devotional *Streams in the Desert* during the days in which her husband, Charles, was slowly dying from heart failure, a complication brought on by his intense missionary zeal. She includes as the April 1st devotional the following poem by Annie Johnson Flint:

"I Will Not Doubt"

I will not doubt, though all my ships at sea
Come drifting home with broken masts and sails,
I will believe the Hand which never fails,
From seeming evil worketh good for me.
And though I weep because those sails are tattered,
Still will I cry, while my best hopes lie shattered:
"I trust in Thee."

I will not doubt, though all my prayers return
Unanswered from the still, white realm above;
I will believe it is an all-wise love
Which has refused these things for which I yearn;
And though at times I cannot keep from grieving,
Yet the pure ardor of my fixed believing
Undimmed shall burn.

I will not doubt, though sorrows fall like rain,
And troubles swarm like bees about a hive.
I will believe the heights for which I strive
Are only reached by anguish and by pain;
And though I groan and writhe beneath my crosses
I yet shall see through my severest losses
The greater gain.

I will not doubt. Well anchored in this faith,
Like some staunch ship, my soul braves every gale;
So strong its courage that it will not quail
To breast the mighty unknown sea of death.
Oh, may I cry, though body parts with spirit,
"I do not doubt," so listening worlds may hear it,
With my last breath.[18]

Reflection and Application

1. If Jesus had lived his life trying to avoid suffering, what would his life have been like? Were there times when Jesus sought to suffer? How and why did suffering come to Jesus?

2. What is your theology of suffering? "If there were a good God, he would not let this happen!" How do you answer this argument against the existence of God? Is there any suffering in your experience that hinders your trust in God?

3. Paul Billheimer writes,

   > God's primary occupation in this age is not regulating the universe by "the mighty power of his command," but it is teaching the members of His Bride-elect the lessons of agape love in preparation for the throne. He is doing nothing in the realm of redemption that is not related to this task. Therefore every single incident, whether of joy or sorrow, bane or blessing, pain or pleasure, without exception is being utilized by God for the purpose of procuring the members of His Bridehood and maturing them in agape love. Thus, the supreme purpose of life on earth is not pleasure, fame, wealth, or any other form of worldly success, but learning agape love.[19]

   Do you agree or disagree with this statement? Why? What do you like about Billheimer's statement? What do you dislike about Billheimer's statement?

4. What is one thought you can take from this chapter to reflect upon in the days ahead with the guidance of the Holy Spirit? What is one prayer over which you will spend time with the Lord?

5

Forgiven

The first thing God wants to do for us is to give us His gift of grace and forgiveness. Even among the people of God, I find a lot of people who live with great guilt. We will never develop into what God wants us to be until we find out what it means to have God's forgiveness. That forgiveness is a gracious gift that we can never earn. In fact, there is nothing we can do to receive it except to take it from His hand in repentant faith.

—Dennis Kinlaw

At the heart of the Christian faith is the transformation of a person into what he or she was created to be, being made into an eternal child of God. Our sin and rebellion separates us from God, but he redeems us through the work of Jesus on the cross, forgiving our sins and our sin nature. Forgiveness is an act of pure grace from God. There is a granting and acceptance of forgiveness; it is offered as a gift by God, and the offender responds in repentance. The effect of forgiveness is to restore the relationship that was broken by sin, a complete removal of the hostility and alienation between God and the one forgiven (Isa. 38:17; Jer. 31:34; Micah 7:19). There is nothing a sinner needs more than forgiveness, than to hear the words, "Your sins are forgiven."

Psalm 32:1 proclaims the wonder of redemption, "Oh, what joy for those whose disobedience is forgiven, whose sin is put out of sight!" The psalmist recognized the life-changing joy that comes when we are able to live in the assurance of forgiveness. It frees us to live in a new way. But this state of joy isn't entered into or retained automatically. It needs to be embraced, understood, nurtured, and refreshed. And for some, although they hear words of forgiveness, the joy that comes remains elusive. As in all aspects of our relationship with God, our faith is at issue. This leads us to ask what is required for a steadfast faith in God's forgiveness. How might we live with a growing faith in the assurance of this grace? What is the courageous faith that will help us embrace God's forgiveness and live as forgiven children?

Faith and trust are intertwined in all of our relationships. For us to trust someone, we must see that person as worthy of or appropriate for trust. We need to have faith in their truthfulness, their strength and ability to respond to trust, and their goodness with which they respond with fidelity. Do we hold firmly to this faith in our relationship with God? Accepting the truthfulness of God and his ability to do what he wills (his omnipotence), let's dig deeper into God's goodness as part of the foundation for our trust. Here are a couple of definitions that may help. The Merriam-Webster Dictionary defines "faith" in terms of allegiance to duty or person, fidelity, and specifically, belief and trust in and loyalty to God. Immediately we see common ground between faith and trust. They go hand in hand with trust being defined as "assured reliance on the character, ability, strength, or truth of someone or something." When the God/human relationship first began, faith and trust were at its core. God gave Adam and Eve one command and asked that they trust him.

Is our faith in the goodness of God as deep as it can be and as settled as it needs to be? This faith has carried some through very dark times. God graciously reveals more than enough about himself to assure us of his goodness and tells us that he holds our very best in his heart, i.e., at the center of his will. The church has come to its understanding of the goodness of God over millennia in which it has sought with finite minds to comprehend the perfection of God, which includes his goodness. Here are a few of our basic beliefs:

- "If holiness is perfect goodness, it includes within it already the idea of perfect being, which Anselm defined as 'that than which nothing greater can be conceived.'"[1]
- "God remains always constant with his own nature as insurmountably good."[2]
- "God's essential nature does not change from better to worse, but remains always only the best."[3]
- "The divine goodness is that attribute through which God wills the happiness of creatures and desires to impart to creatures all the goodness they are capable of receiving."[4]
- "That God is love implies that benevolent affection, good will, and empathic understanding are the characteristic qualities in God through which God relates compassionately to creatures."[5]

These are long-accepted beliefs about the eternal goodness of God. They tell us we can trust God to forgive. We are not left, though, with only the lofty words of scholars for our belief in the goodness of God. The almighty Creator of the universe takes on a description of himself that speaks volumes, a description very familiar to all of us. As Jesus by his life and ministry reveals much about the character of God, his own words give us this description. This is the most interesting and important term in the Gospels for reflecting how Jesus thought about God, the simple word "Father." This is revelation! In the Old Testament, God is occasionally thought of as Father, but the term is usually used of God's relationship to Israel as a people, not of his relationship to individuals.

In the New Testament, though, the name occurs in reference to God in the Gospel of Mark four times, in the Gospel of Matthew thirty-six times, and in the Gospel of John one hundred times. In the Pauline letters the description of God as Father occurs forty times.[6] Jesus' relationship to God as his Father is one he knows directly and innately, and into which he invites his disciples. Among the most notable of his statements reflecting this Father/Son relationship is Matthew 11:27: "All things have been handed over to me by my Father; and no one knows the Son except the Father, and no one knows the Father except the Son and anyone to whom the Son chooses to reveal him" (NRSV). These statements identifying God as his Father were revolutionary, enough to cause the Jewish leaders to accuse Jesus of blasphemy and to plot to kill him (John 10:22–38). Even today, it is not unusual for someone to feel surprised upon first hearing that Jesus tells us we may refer to God as our Father. God reveals himself as our Father who gives good gifts (Luke 11:13), including the gift of forgiveness.

Jesus went even further. The word *father* can describe a relationship that is little more than biological. There are many children who have little or no knowledge of their father. The name can also be applied to a relationship that is distant, awkward, or cold. Jesus did not allow for these thoughts to be brought in as descriptive of God as Father. The pinnacle was reached when he used the name *Abba* to refer to God and he gives his disciples the privilege of doing the same. "Abba" is an Aramaic word, an intimate word used by children when speaking to their father. Adults might also use the term in the intimacy of the family relationship. With its reference to God, Jesus signals a radically new understanding of both his relationship with God and ours.

Indeed, Joachim Jeremias discovered that the Jews in Jesus' time avoided applying the word *abba* to God. "We do not have a single example of God being addressed as 'abba' in Judaism."[7] While we only have record of Jesus using the title in the garden of Gethsemane, Paul's use of the term in Romans 8:15 and Galatians 4:6 reflect the early Christian practice of prayer, a practice in which God was addressed as Abba. From Jesus' time forward, God may be called Abba. "This represents the attitude Christians are to have toward God. They are to approach Him with all the openness and confidence and affection of small children."[8] You and I may call God *Abba*!

Thus, based on creation, his provision for our needs, his identification of himself as our Abba Father, and especially his self-sacrificial sending of his Son, we have a compelling reason to commit to the goodness of God. We can trust him because he is not a distant deity but our loving, intimate Father. This is what he reveals about himself, and it is our assurance for his call to us to trust him for our forgiveness. It is not sufficient, though, that we merely acknowledge this as a theological premise. It must move from our head to our heart so that it has profound impact on our lives. We must really believe it! Almighty God, the creator of a trillion galaxies, is our loving Father.

Full understanding of this is beyond our finite minds. And though we should be growing in our understanding, there are things that can cause a person to hear and yet not accept this image of God at all. Some simply do not give their faith enough attention to even think about what the relationship really offers. They may think of God as a celestial watchmaker who created the world and set it in motion, then left it to follow its own course. For others, a distorted image of God as an angry deity—distant, judgmental, and demanding—may prevent them from embracing this revelation. Some people struggle with a poor image of their earthly father, which adversely affects their view of their heavenly Father. Studies have shown that attachment to fathers predicts attachment to God.[9] Brennan Manning writes,

> It is always true to some extent that we make our images of God. It is even truer that our image of God makes us. Eventually we become like the God we image. One of the most beautiful

> fruits of knowing the God of Jesus is a compassionate attitude toward ourselves. . . . This is why Scripture attaches such importance to *knowing* God. Healing our image of God heals our image of ourselves.[10]

Knowing God as a good Father undercuts simplistic and inaccurate notions about his character. True knowledge of God helps us accept our forgiveness and live in the joy that comes with it. Dennis Kinlaw writes,

> The first thing God wants to do for us is to give us his gift of grace and forgiveness. Even among the people of God, I find a lot of people who live with great guilt. We will never develop into what God wants us to be until we find out what it means to have God's forgiveness. That forgiveness is a gracious gift that we can never earn. In fact, there is nothing we can do to receive it except to take it from his hand in repentant faith. When we have accepted his gift, we are on our way to grace and growth. . . .
>
> Tragically, I have seen some people who cannot accept this gift. But we will never know any further growth or grace until we can say that our sins are nailed to his Cross and that we are forgiven and free.[11]

God *wants* to give us grace and forgiveness. But truly accepting love, forgiveness, and healing can be harder than giving it. One of the great challenges of the spiritual life is accepting God's forgiveness as a gift. It goes against our desire for self-sufficiency and a deeply held belief that we have to have merit before we can receive something. We hear this in many churches where the message goes like this: God is good; you are bad; try harder. By our nature we want to fix things, then maybe God will bless us, and maybe even like us. But as David Benner writes, "Spiritual transformation does not result from fixing our problems. It results from turning to God in the midst of them and meeting God just as we are. Turning to God is the core of prayer. Turning to God in our sin and shame is the heart of spiritual transformation."[12] James Byron Smith writes, "In my search of Scripture I was unable to find a passage in which Jesus tells us that God only likes us when we're good or when we engage in pious activities. Instead he tells of a God who offers unconditional acceptance to all people."[13] The first thing that God wants from us is not improved moral behavior, but a loving response to his love.

Another obstacle to consider is shame, which may hinder our acceptance of forgiveness. Shame can be a severe impediment to accepting and enjoying one's status as a forgiven child. While Western cultures are more guilt-oriented and Eastern cultures more shame-oriented, everyone can and does experience shame in some form. It plays a significant role in our lives and thus needs to be understood and transformed by truth. Shame is a negative state arising from feelings of failure to live up to someone's expectations or ideals. It always arises out of a relational context and will produce emotions of condemnation, rejection, abandonment, betrayal, and humiliation. Some, because of a sense of shame, cannot allow the freedom of forgiveness to become real. "The way I have lived, why would God listen to me? Why would God want to forgive me?"*

Shame can block our full acceptance of forgiveness and stunt our growth in intimacy with our Father. Guilt and shame are related but significantly different. Guilt is about a law broken, the focus being on the behavior. Shame, on the other hand, is a value judgment on the self. Guilt says, "I have done something wrong." Shame generates the "ongoing premise that one is fundamentally bad, inadequate, defective, unworthy, or not fully valid as a human being."[14] Left unchecked, shame can produce a debilitating sense of personal inadequacy, as well as a sense that this inadequacy is known and is being judged by others.[15]

Our enemy Satan uses shame to deceive us, getting us to focus on past failures and bad choices so the emphasis is on what we have done rather than what God wants to do. Shame inherently separates us from God because it causes us to try to hide, and this is crippling. Looking once again at the creation story, we see that this human malady extends as far back as Adam and Eve. Having disobeyed the one command given them by God, they were ashamed when

---

*This brief consideration of shame is not presented as a solution or cure. The problem can be very deep, and may call for professional counseling for some. The desire is that this discussion may create an awareness that will take us to the Lord in prayer, asking for the guidance and molding of the Holy Spirit in our lives. It could also create an awareness of the presence of shame in others and help us to be open to be used by the Lord in their lives.

God confronted them. They hid themselves, both physically and by their action of deflecting blame (Gen. 3:8). "When persons feel unacceptable, they avoid acknowledging responsibility for behaviors that might reveal their unacceptability."[16] Unable to take responsibility for what they had done, Adam and Eve tried to blame others. Adam was first, pointing to his wife as the one who was at fault. Eve followed, pointing at the serpent as the one to blame. Interestingly, we see no repentance and request for forgiveness, only excuses. When they had every reason and opportunity to turn to God for forgiveness, shame blocked the way. But even so, we see God immediately attending to their needs, confirming what we are holding as true about his character. This response of God reminds us that "their disobedience is not the final word in defining who they are. First and foremost, they are God's creatures."[17]

Jesus' story about the prodigal son, a story familiar to many of us, offers a lesson on shame and forgiveness. Jesus tells of a father and two sons, the younger of whom asked for his inheritance, even while his father was still alive. This was a great dishonor to his father, but the father complied with the request. The son took the money and moved to a foreign land where he wasted it in wild, dishonorable living. Soon this son found himself penniless and starving, feeding a farmer's pigs in this foreign country in order to survive. Jesus uses what happens next to illustrate the scope of the grace and forgiveness our Father in heaven holds for us. Jesus says of this son, "When he finally came to his senses, he said to himself, 'At home even the hired servants have food enough to spare, and here I am dying of hunger! I will go home to my father and say, "Father,

I have sinned against both heaven and you, and I am no longer worthy of being called your son. Please take me on as a hired servant'"" (Luke 15:17–19).

His sin had destroyed his sense of self-worth, his worth as a son. "I am no longer worthy." A powerful shame kept him in the pig pen, where he continued the humiliating work. He was hiding in his shame and it kept him separated from his father. Only when he came to his senses and glimpsed the possibilities in his relationship with his father was he able to start the journey home and allow healing to begin. But even then, his expectation of the relationship was limited to food and the status of a servant. Still thinking of his father's love as conditional, he wondered what kind of reception he would receive when he returned home. He couldn't comprehend the breadth and length and height and depth of the forgiveness his father longed to give to him. Clinging to a sense of worthlessness, he imagined a place for himself far below that which belongs to a son.[18] But he was about to experience the true character of his father, which Jesus uses to reveal the true heart of our Father. Jesus continues,

> "So he returned home to his father. And while he was still a long way off, his father saw him coming. Filled with love and compassion, he ran to his son, embraced him, and kissed him. His son said to him, 'Father, I have sinned against both heaven and you, and I am no longer worthy of being called your son.'
>
> "But his father said to the servants, 'Quick! Bring the finest robe in the house and put it on

> him. Get a ring for his finger and sandals for his feet. And kill the calf we have been fattening. We must celebrate with a feast, for this son of mine was dead and has now returned to life. He was lost, but now he is found.' So the party began." (Luke 15:20–24)

The son was home, a place of belonging and acceptance. Our true home is the place where we are the closest to God. It's a place where forgiven sins need not separate. Leaving home, as the prodigal did, is "a denial of the spiritual reality that I belong to God with every part of my being, that God holds me safe in an eternal embrace . . ."[19] To surrender to divine love and return home is to find our soul's home, "the place and identity for which we yearn in every cell of our being."[20] Home is a place of affirmation. When Jesus was baptized, he heard the words of his Father saying, "This is my dearly loved Son, who brings me great joy" (Matt. 3:17). Accepting the forgiveness God offers puts us in this place where we, too, can hear the voice saying, "You are my beloved child." After his baptism, Jesus was led into the wilderness where the temptations sought to seduce him to turn away from this voice. God had said, "You are my beloved." How different from the wilderness. The false voices in our wilderness say, "Prove that you are worthy of being loved."

What happened in the days after the prodigal returned? We hope he lived a fulfilling life of gratitude in which his deepest desire was to honor his father. But the parable does not provide a happy-ever-after ending. That is not its purpose. Instead, it invites us to put ourselves in the place of the prodigal son, to ask what he faced that we, too, are facing. These are not just big things. We can keep a whole trash bin of little things that keep telling us we are less than who we really are in Christ. Although our particular situations will vary considerably, we are all confronted by one of life's hardest of spiritual choices: to trust or not to trust in the sufficiency of God's goodness, in the intimacy of God as Abba Father, and live within the context of that unconditional love. This is the crux of courageous faith, a faith that rejects limits on God's goodness and forgiveness; a faith that determines to seek first the kingdom of God, which is our home. God's grace can lead us to decide we want to live as a beloved child and God's grace can be transforming us as the reality of that life becomes more and more who we are. Discovering that our Father's mercies are new every morning, we are invited each day to a rhythm of new and deeper intimacy. Benner writes, "As we see how deeply loved we are by God—in our depths, complexity, totality and sinfulness—we dare to allow God more complete access to the dark parts of our soul that most need transformation. And God precedes us on this journey, waiting to meet us in the depths of our self."[21] Courageous faith trusts in the goodness of God, Abba Father, and is determined to press on into that relationship, letting neither one's past nor the recriminations of the wilderness deny us the joys of a forgiven child. Now, how do we live with this status? How will a deeper embrace of our Father's loving forgiveness change our lives?

Reflection and Application

1. What is the difference between guilt and shame? How are the consequences of the two different?

2. Reflect on your *knowing* of God's love, God's character, and your understanding of who God is. How much does this knowing form the foundation of your life? Can it be more? In what ways do you experience divine love? How do you know it to be true even when you do not sense it?

3. Is there an area of your life in which it is difficult for you to trust God's forgiveness? Examine this area and test it against what Scripture says about God. What step can you take to move beyond this difficulty?

4. There are many self-help remedies in our world today that point people to sources of well-being other than God. Is there a story of God's forgiveness that you know that you may be/should be able to use to help another trying to understand the forgiveness of God?

5. What is one thought you can take from this chapter to reflect upon in the days ahead with the guidance of the Holy Spirit? What is one prayer over which you will spend time with the Lord?

6

Forgiving

In a single, silent moment, his rage, his fear, his humiliation and helplessness, had fallen away. That morning, he believed, he was a new creation. Softly, he wept . . . At that moment, something shifted sweetly inside him. It was forgiveness, beautiful and effortless and complete. For Louie Zamperini, the war was over.

—Laura Hillenbrand

What is there in your faith that allows you to forgive others? "The faithful love of the Lord never ends! His mercies never cease. Great is his faithfulness; his mercies begin afresh each morning" (Lam. 3:22–23). Interesting words to be found in a book called Lamentations. I am often mindful of the Lord's mercies, which include being spared the personal trauma of a serious crime. So, it was something of a shock when Sam spoke in our Friday morning men's group about having to forgive the man who murdered his seventeen-year-old son. Sam later shared the story. His son Kyle had joined an informal outreach that started with the objective of giving at-risk teenagers a home where they could hang out and avoid the temptation of drugs. Two guys lived in the house and there was frequent parental supervision with a strict rule of no drugs. One tragic night, three men on a drug binge went to the house in the mistaken belief they would be able to buy drugs. Things got ugly when they were forced to leave. The three went to a local store where they bought a gun and ammo, then returned to the house. When their drug-induced spree was over, three innocent people were left critically wounded and four were dead, including Sam's son.

Through the numbness that immediately sets in after news of this severity comes, Sam knew he was seeing the horrible face of this fallen world. He began reaching out for something to answer the questions that follow. What now? How does a person respond to something like this? He found comfort in reports that Kyle had acted bravely in the defense of others. There was comfort from church members who immediately came around to help. Of greatest comfort was the sense that when Kyle died he fell into the loving arms of Jesus. And Sam began to glimpse the hand of God in the midst of horror. As a regular listener to Christian radio, he knew the Lord had something for him when he heard a message on anger and forgiveness just two days after the crime. Incredibly, his journey of forgiveness had already begun. Sam says he didn't wrestle with forgiveness. As the Holy Spirit worked in his heart, forgiveness just flowed in. He knew this was an opportunity to be obedient. He knew this was God. The tremendous pain persisted and there was still the nagging question about why this had happened, but in the midst of this there was and remains a sense of peace and calm that comes only from the God of peace. In the years that have followed, Sam has shared his story with others. His obedience in his ongoing journey of forgiveness helps us to ask, "What is the forgiveness to which we are called? How does God forgive? How do we forgive?" Sam's story helps us find answers to some of life's toughest questions.

Most people have been at least somewhat exposed to the idea that it is good to forgive. "To err is human, to forgive divine." But even with general acknowledgment of benefit coming from forgiveness, the rational mind may find many reasons to resist forgiving. The more reasonable course of action may seem to be for the offended party to opt for repayment, revenge, and resentment. Those choices seem to satisfy a longing of the fallen self. As appealing as these may seem, though, none of them work; none of them provide the healing the injury requires. "Repayment is impossible. Revenge is impotent. Resentment is impractical."[1]

In an interview on *60 Minutes*, a woman told of her reaction to the drunk driver who killed her younger brother. She felt the only emotion the man deserved was hate. She made it her mission to find all the incriminating evidence she could and to do everything within her power to see that he got the maximum possible sentence, the maximum possible pain. Looking back on that time, she realizes she was locked in a prison of her own making, sentenced to a life of vengeance. Her self-assessment was that she had become a terrible mother, a terrible teacher, and an uninspiring person. Only after meeting face-to-face with the perpetrator through a program of restorative justice was she able to forgive and be released herself. As unnatural as it may seem, it is forgiveness that heals and restores.[2]

The instructions of Jesus frame forgiveness in a way quite different from the world. Forgiveness is part of the image of God and of our design in his image. It is at the heart of God's work among humanity. God created us to be in a personal relationship with him, but that relationship was broken by the evil we call sin. Sin always calls for repentance and requires God's offer of redemption through forgiveness. God in grace heals his creation through forgiveness. The whole essence of Jesus' life is that in him we see clearly displayed the attitude of God to mankind. Now that attitude was the very reverse of what we had thought God's attitude to be. It was not an attitude of stern, severe, austere justice—not an attitude of continual demand. It was an attitude of perfect love, of a heart yearning with love and eager to forgive.[3]

Scripture provides many instructions for our attitude toward others, an attitude that is to be a reflection of God's attitude toward us. When Jesus gave us the Great Commandment, he first spoke of our love for God. Then he expanded this by adding a second *equally important* part, "Love your neighbor as yourself" (Matt. 22:39). On these, Jesus said, the entire law and all the demands of the prophets are based (Matt. 22:40). This means this is the guiding principle for all of life for a follower of Jesus. It is the keystone for understanding and applying the command to forgive. We are to seek for our neighbor nothing less than the relationship with God that we desire for ourselves. We are to forgive, and to seek an offender's highest good.

Prominence is given to forgiveness by its inclusion in the Lord's Prayer. When the disciples asked Jesus to teach them to pray, he included an act of love—forgiveness—in his prayer: "... and forgive us our sins, as we have forgiven those who sin against us" (Matt. 6:12). It is clear that Jesus' expectation for his disciples is that as we are forgiven we will forgive others, that we will be forgiven forgivers. To this was added these potent words, "If you forgive those who sin against you, your heavenly Father will forgive you. But if you refuse to forgive others, your Father will not forgive your sins" (Matt. 6:14–15).

This warning has caused many a reader to pause. Let's be clear in our understanding of what is meant. It is unmistakable that a direct connection exists between God's forgiveness and our forgiveness. This warning can seem to say that only after you forgive those who sin against you will God offer his forgiveness to you. But the message of the prayer is not about payment to God. If we fail to forgive, we are disobedient. As long as we remain unforgiving, we are unrepentant and cannot receive the forgiveness that God has for us for that sin of unforgiveness. Our lack of forgiveness of another hinders our relationship with God and God's forgiveness of us.

So, how are we to forgive? When every instinct pulls us to be our worst, how do we become our best? The challenge of forgiving can seem even greater as the command is explained. How? "[J]ust as God through Christ has forgiven you" (Eph. 4:32). Jesus, of course, lived out his commands and is our model for living out these instructions. The pinnacle of teaching on forgiveness is the prayer of Jesus from the cross for those who were crucifying him, "Father, forgive them" (Luke 23:34). Paul carried Jesus' teaching forward, "Make allowance for each other's faults, and forgive anyone who offends you. Remember, the Lord forgave you, so you must forgive others" (Col. 3:13). A starting point for forgiving is to remember we are forgiven.

I can read these words and quickly pass over them without really applying them to myself. Sometimes it seems impossible to forgive. Sometimes we just don't want to forgive. Sometimes we just don't want to think about it. We are inclined to set limits to our obligations. We want a line to be drawn so our obligations will cease. "After all," we say, "we're only human!" Interestingly, though, when Scripture sets the standard for forgiving others, that standard is not what can be done humanly. Peter was exhibiting a heart growing in Christlikeness when he asked Jesus how many times he should forgive someone who had sinned against him. His suggestion of seven times more than doubled the rabbinical formula that one should not ask the forgiveness of a neighbor more than three times. Still, Peter wanted the Lord to draw a line in the matter of forgiveness. Then he could measure it, control it, and perhaps it would be within his ability. Peter must have been shocked by Jesus' answer, which moved forgiveness from a mechanical mathematical equation to an attitude of the heart. Jesus taught of unlimited forgiveness (Matt. 18:21–22).

So, what is this forgiveness, this attitude of the heart, to which we are called? First, consider what it is not. It is not merely summoning up warm feelings for whomever has offended. It is not cheap grace that treats sin as if it is unimportant and irrelevant. Sin is not excusable, but is always forgivable. So, forgiveness doesn't say it was just an accident, or you must be overstressed, or you have been treated poorly. To forgive isn't to shrug off or condone. So, what is it? How are we to understand forgiveness? One critique of concepts of forgiveness common in Western culture divides them between *legal* and *psychological*. Legal forgiveness is simply the forswearing of revenge or forgoing justified retributive action. Such forgiveness might be offered for reasons of convenience or because it produces the best consequences for oneself. In other words, in a balance of the pros and cons, forgiveness seems more beneficial overall. It serves one's self-interest to just "forgive" and move on.

Psychological forgiveness is an improvement over legal forgiveness because it calls for a refusal to hold on to emotions such as anger, hatred, or resentment, but it is still flawed:

> Views that claim to speak of forgiveness but speak only of emotional change that can be instrumentally motivated fail to live up to their aspirations; they are not speaking of forgiveness. Forgiveness may well be therapeutic in various ways and at certain times, but to major in that theme suggests a lack of appropriate confrontation with the culpable evil to which forgiveness responds and a problematic indifference to moral injuries. Getting over my anger might help open a way forward for a relationship with the person who was the object of that anger, but it might also fail to aim at or contribute to an appropriate relationship.[4]

In other words, psychological forgiveness is motivated by the emotional benefit it may bring *to the one who is forgiving*. The flaw shared by both the legal and psychological conceptions of forgiveness is their self-reference. It is a self-help remedy to serve oneself. Neither deals with the wrongdoing or the wrongdoer but seeks merely to get beyond them. Neither seeks the moral restoration of the offender. They approach forgiveness from the standpoint of change on the part of the victim. Neither is forgiveness in the image of God's forgiveness.

The forgiving to which the follower of Jesus is called, essential to Christian discipleship, is to condemn the fault and spare the wrongdoer. It is to name the wrong and condemn it, then to give the wrongdoer, in the name of Christ, "the gift of not counting the wrongdoing against them."[5] Forgiveness is the Great Commandment in action, loving our neighbor and desiring his or her best because that is what our Father has done for us. "Forgiveness is motivated by divine love and calls offenders back to that love."[6] More than how we feel about an offender, forgiveness is about how we treat them. It is more related to an act of our will than to our emotions. The dilemma we face here may call to mind the cry of the father, "I do believe [an act of his will], but help me overcome my unbelief [prayer for help in the process]!" (Mark 9:24). So we might pray, "I forgive [an act of our will]; conform my heart to your forgiving heart [prayer for the process]." Love, in this context, is an action. Loving our enemies is the only way to really overcome our enemies. There is no power in the universe able to conquer evil other than love.

True forgiveness asks the difficult question, "How in this situation am I totally available to God for the sake of the other?" It addresses the evil that is responsible for the broken relationship, an evil called sin. It is a forgiveness that "overcomes sin by healing sinners and restoring them to good."[7] Being about the other, "the primary issue is not inner peace for oneself, not moral rightness with one's own conscience, not assurance of one's salvation. These are self-centered, narcissistic goals . . ."[8] True forgiveness, concludes Augsburger, is really about regaining a brother or a sister. "Forgiveness overcomes evil with good. Forgiveness mirrors the generosity of God whose ultimate goal is neither to satisfy injured pride nor to justly apportion reward and punishment, but to free sinful humanity from evil and thereby reestablish communion with us."[9] To the extent we are able, we do as God does.

Practical steps for those seeking to forgive in this manner are offered in the Bible. Those seeking to forgive should imitate Jesus, who did not retaliate when he was insulted. He left his case in the hands of God (1 Peter 2:23). They do not seek revenge, rather, they remember that vengeance is the responsibility of God (Rom. 12:19). Scripture admonishes, "Bless those who persecute you. Don't curse them; pray that God will bless them" (Rom. 12:14). They avoid cursing their enemy, both inwardly and outwardly. They pray for them, bestowing a blessing upon them. They also initiate the process of forgiveness. In the midst of a culture steeped in ritual sacrifices, Jesus taught that reconciliation is more important than the offer of the sacrifices. Even if one is standing at the altar making a sacrifice, if he remembers a conflict he is to go and seek reconciliation, then return to offer the sacrifice to God (Matt. 5:23–24).

Let's be clear and allow no false piety to enter into what we are saying. The hurts that resist forgiveness can come in the full range from slight injury to devastation. They often come from an attack on dignity, a dehumanizing and devaluing encounter suffered at the hands of fallen people in a fallen world. For us to properly respond to the command of forgiveness, especially when the alternatives seem so natural, rational, and appealing, is an immense task. Forgiveness pits a seemingly rational choice (e.g., repayment, revenge, resentment) against Jesus' example of forgiveness. The model is clear; the rational and emotional nature of a person resists. In the admittedly complex dynamics of forgiveness, we know that we are not enough on our own for the task, but we are not left alone. As a part of our spiritual formation, we remember that our ability to forgive is first and foremost a work of the Holy Spirit.* There is enough love and enough power in the cross of Christ to enable us to forget past hurts and continue our relationships as if there had never been anything wrong. Even with the best intentions, this will never be done in human strength; only the Spirit of Jesus can enable us to forget our pains and hurts.[10]

Paul challenged the Galatians to remember that *being in Christ* allowed them to participate in the fruit of the Spirit (5:16–26). "His rejoinder reminds us that when we live by the Spirit we will be enabled to love our neighbors, to bless others rather than curse them, and to empower others rather than dominate them."[11] The work of the

---

*See *The Quest for Holiness, From Shallow Belief to Mature Believer,* chapters 5 and 6, for a more detailed discussion of the work of the Holy Spirit.

Holy Spirit may come both in ways that are supernatural, beyond our understanding, and in ways that we can come to understand such as simply helping us understand the righteousness of God's ways.

On occasion, the Holy Spirit works to immediately bring a person to forgiveness. The book *Unbroken* tells the story of Louie Zamperini, a prisoner of the Japanese during WWII. Before the war, Zamperini had been an Olympic athlete, one of the fastest milers in the world and expected someday to hold the world record. With the onset of the war he enlisted in the Army Air Corp and was taken prisoner after being shot down on a mission in the Pacific theater. The prison camp was harsh and inhumane at its best, but Zamperini was singled out as the target of especially harsh treatment by a sadistic guard nicknamed "the Bird." He endured endless torment and degrading assaults on his dignity. Even after his liberation and return to the United States, Zamperini carried with him hatred and a desire for revenge.

Though the war had been over for many years, it continued every day for Zamperini. His life was broken and in a downward spiral that was destroying him, his family, and everything around him. It was God's grace that Billy Graham was holding a crusade in Los Angeles during this time. Zamperini at first rejected the urging of his wife to attend, then went reluctantly, sitting in a place where he could make a quick exit when the message became unacceptable. However, the unexpected happened. Zamperini opened his heart to Jesus and was flooded with healing and renewal, so much so that he was able to come to the point of forgiving the Bird.

> In a single, silent moment, his rage, his fear, his humiliation and helplessness, had fallen away. That morning, he believed, he was a new creation. Softly, he wept . . . At that moment, something shifted sweetly inside him. It was forgiveness, beautiful and effortless and complete. For Louie Zamperini, the war was over.[12]

Zamperini's release from the bondage of unforgiveness came in an instant. More often, forgiveness comes over time, more of a process than a once-and-for-all decision, as a byproduct of a healing process. Corrie ten Boom spoke candidly about her experience with forgiveness. She and her sister Betsie were sent to the Ravensbrück concentration camp for hiding Jews during WWII. Betsie died as a result of the inhumane treatment of prisoners in the camp. After the war, Corrie began to speak of forgiveness and healing in both her native Holland and in Germany. She recalls the evening when, after speaking on forgiveness, she saw a man coming toward her. Though he did not recognize her, she recognized him. He confirmed that he had been one of the guards at Ravensbrück. "But since that time," he said, "I have become a Christian. I know that God has forgiven me for the cruel things I did there, but I would like to hear it from your lips as well. *Fräulein* . . . will you forgive me?" It seemed to Corrie like hours that the former guard stood there with his hand extended. She wrestled with the most difficult thing she ever had to do, but she knew she must forgive.

> And still I stood there with the coldness clutching my heart. But forgiveness is not an emotion—I

> knew that too. Forgiveness is an act of the will, and the will can function regardless of the temperature of the heart. "Jesus, help me!" I prayed silently. "I can lift my hand. I can do that much. You supply the feeling." And so woodenly, mechanically, I thrust my hand into the one stretched out to me. And as I did, an incredible thing took place. The current started in my shoulder, raced down my arm, sprang into our joined hands. And then this healing warmth seemed to flood my whole being, bringing tears to my eyes. "I forgive you, brother!" I cried. "With all my heart!" For a long moment we grasped each other's hands, the former guard and the former prisoner. I had never known God's love so intensely as I did then.[13]

Corrie shares another valuable lesson. She thought that having learned to forgive in that hardest of situations, she would never again have difficulty in forgiving. But that was not so. Forgiveness can become a lifestyle, but its power must be drawn fresh from God each day.

Let's dig a little deeper into the notion that forgiveness may be more related to an act of our will than our emotions. Look at the forgiveness for which Jesus prayed on the cross. In that account, there are no emotions of warm feelings or affection for the soldiers who were crucifying him, but as an act of his will Jesus was able to seek their very best, to ask the Father to forgive them. "We like to think that Jesus spoke with compassion, but he may well have spit these words out. He was human enough to feel all the recrimination to which he was entitled, and he too wrestled with the unnatural character of forgiveness."[14]

We can learn more from this by remembering that this forgiveness for which Jesus prayed was not cheap or easy forgiveness. Jesus' humanity was real and it was painfully and horribly assaulted on the cross. If we think his words of forgiveness were possible only because of his divinity, we can write them off as impossible for us. But he suffered in his humanity, and his words cannot be dismissed.

We often hear the common admonition to "forgive and forget." For both Louie Zamperini and Corrie ten Boom, we see the forgiveness but know they could never forget. Hopefully we have gained some ground in understanding what it means to forgive, but what about forgetting? Perhaps the ideal is that eventually, when the time is ripe, we allow an offense to slip into oblivion. Certainly *forgetting* conveys the understanding that we are not to continue with a grudge. As John Henry Jowett writes,

> My forgiveness of my brother is to be complete. No sullenness is to remain, no sulky temper which so easily gives birth to thunder and lightning. There is to be no painful aloofness, no assumption of a superiority which rains contempt upon the offenders. When I forgive, I am not to carry any gunpowder forward on the journey. I am to empty out all my explosives, all my ammunition of anger and revenge, I am not to "bear a grudge." (Lev. 19:18).[15]

But we should not pursue a goal of *forgetting* that would trivialize forgiveness, and this is especially true for deep hurts. It is a process of prayer and surrender to the work of the Holy Spirit forming in us the ability to will the well-being of both the victim and the violator, conforming our will to the will of our Father.

> "Letting go" finally, does not mean letting go of reality. It does mean that, through prayer, we let ourselves go into the arms of God whose knowledge is superior but whose ability to will the well-being of all involved is greater as well. In those arms we are held—not to be carried away from our pain, but to be carried through it. Just as the resurrected Jesus bore the marks of the nail prints . . . "the future made possible for us through forgiveness is not 'as if the sin never happened,' but a future marked precisely in and through the scars of our experiences."[16]

Though reconciliation may be the final step in forgiveness, that is not always the case. If the soldiers around the cross repented and accepted the forgiveness offered by the Father at the request of the Son, we can only imagine the joy of the reconciliation that would follow. But that reconciliation, if it happened, took place in heaven. Forgiveness does not put us in a place where we should expect to find fulfillment in and from the one forgiven. That may happen, but it certainly is not guaranteed, nor is it a proper motive for forgiving. Rather, forgiving frees us to look to our Father as the true source of our fulfilled self. We do not primarily forgive in order to restore our relationship with the one who is forgiven. We forgive to restore our relationship with our Father in heaven. It is the image of the Father to forgive. In forgiving, we are restored to that image.

Jesus' forgiveness from the cross is viewed by many as the supreme example of forgiveness. That this act seems so far above the natural human inclination points to how difficult it is for a disciple of Jesus to follow that forgiveness in his or her life. Yet, God's grace seeks a total transformation for men and women, for they belong to God. His high calling in a believer's life is without compromise. This radical transformation is from an exalted view of self to exaltation of God. It comes with the simple truth that the human vocation on earth is to do the will of God. We should seek to live with this truth uppermost in mind, to see each day and each day's activities in its light, and to trust God to conform our hearts to his will. This is a heart being transformed into the likeness of Christ, the image of God, a heart that can forgive even those who are seeking to crucify.

Reflection and Application

1. What noteworthy acts of forgiveness have you heard about or experienced? What made such forgiveness possible? What was the result of those acts of forgiveness?

2. "We do not primarily forgive in order to restore our relationship with the one who is forgiven. We forgive to restore our relationship with our Father in heaven." Do you agree with this statement? If so, how does it change your understanding of forgiveness?

3. Spend some time in reflection and prayer. What do you need to understand and perhaps more deeply accept about forgiveness? What attitude of forgiveness do you need to develop? Ask the Holy Spirit to reveal resentments that are buried and need to be forgiven. What do you need to abandon to God in order to forgive others? What courageous faith do you need to ask God for in order to have more of the forgiving nature of Jesus? How does forgiveness relate to the commands of Jesus, which have been summarized as being "totally available to God for the sake of others"? Are you resisting? If so, identify and name the source of that resistance.

4. Thinking about the assurance of the love of God, can you hear your Father in heaven saying about you, "This is my beloved child"? Can you hear it loudly and clearly enough that it shapes how you feel about yourself?

5. What is one thought you can take from this chapter to reflect upon in the days ahead with the guidance of the Holy Spirit? What is one prayer over which you will spend time with the Lord?

7

Courageous Faith in Community

"There arose a reasoning among them, which of them should be the greatest" (Luke 9:46). We know who it is that sows this thought in the Christian community. But perhaps we do not bear in mind enough that no Christian community ever comes together without this thought immediately emerging as a seed of discord.

—Dietrich Bonhoeffer

One of the first things we learn in the Bible is that we need relationships. Creation was incomplete while Adam was alone so God provided. For Adam there was Eve, and for Eve there was Adam, and for both there was God. Since that time almost any prayer of thanksgiving has included gratitude for family and friends. We are blessed, and relationships offer to us some of the greatest possibilities for blessings.

However, even after we have accepted God's free gift of grace and are seeking to live as followers of Jesus, we are aware something is often not quite right in our relationships. We are discerning enough to know generally how we should live, what we should do and what we should not do, what attitudes we should have and which we should not have. But there is a problem. As much as we want to do, think, and feel what is right, there are times when we fail. We too often fall short, and we are troubled by it. We are not surprised to find this principle active in the world, but in our church and in our personal lives? Were we to examine ourselves with a discerning eye we might acknowledge that more than just a little is not right. However we describe what is wrong, we live with it daily. A descriptive metaphor for our human race says we are like a bunch of porcupines trying to huddle together for warmth on a cold winter's night. So we ask, "How do we live as faithful followers of Jesus in our community?"

The conflicts we feel are as old as humankind, recognized and described by no less a saint than the apostle Paul (Rom. 7:14–25). In Paul's description we can sense the anguish and hear the turmoil in his words. Importantly, Paul knew the answer is not to give up and be complacent, but to press on in grace toward God's higher calling. The environment for this spiritual formation may from time to time be a place of solitude, but its primary proving ground will be in community. If life has one lesson to teach, it is surely that we cannot live it alone. "Although the Fall has left us disconnected, God created human beings to be communal."[1] In the calling of the disciples we see that Christianity began with a group. It is a faith that calls people together in fellowship, with its task of living with each other and for each other. The Christian community is not and has never been immune to challenging relationships. Still, community and its relationships are fundamental to our way of life.

Human beings bring an assortment of needs into community, needs that range from the basics such as food and safety to higher order needs such as self-respect, self-esteem, and the desire to belong to and be longed for in harmonious community.[2] The satisfaction of these needs is, for the most part, not within oneself. It is in community that these needs are most often realized and their satisfaction sought, and in which we find lessons for living together. Some spiritual lessons are learned only through suffering and others only through dry seasons. Likewise, many lessons of spiritual formation can only be learned in community. Community affords the believer the opportunity to move to a higher level of spiritual maturity. Indeed, it could be said that community is the crucible of spiritual formation in which dross may be removed, a refining process that will leave a more mature disciple of Jesus.

In community all rights may be challenged. This is a reality. As Christians, living in community can be perplexing. It can leave us wondering how we live out our lives. What does it mean to live as a disciple of Jesus in community? In one sense, the answer is pretty straightforward. The purpose of the Christian life is to be like Jesus, to learn how to live in the kingdom of God as Jesus lived. I heard a pastor say that as disciples of Jesus we are continually unlearning the fall and learning to live in the kingdom of God. That's an apt description. But how do we live a God-honoring life in the various encounters of everyday life?

This conversation finds holiness at its center, though the connection might not be readily apparent if we misunderstand holiness. It is critical that we realize that holiness is not just a list of things we do and things we avoid. That's part of it for sure. There are things to be done and things which a follower of Jesus is to avoid, but that's not the essence of a holy life. The Pharisees loved the Ten Commandments and all the dos and don'ts derived from them, but Jesus made it clear that there is more. Jesus did not set aside the law but pointed to a transformation of the heart, here and now, in keeping the law. Jesus' message that was so violently opposed by the Pharisees and teachers of the law was that true worship of God comes from the heart, not ritual and ceremony.

To be holy *is* to be set apart, but set apart to be different from the destructive nature of the world that dishonors God and damages his creation. In a holy life God has first place and the welfare of others takes precedence over self-serving desires. It grows out of a deepening trust that God is sovereign, good, and holy. It is to love God and his creation, including oneself and others. It is a way of being that loves God for the sake of others and in which we seek to be redemptive agents through whom the love of God enters the world. A holy life is one through which the image (character) of God, as incompletely as it may be formed in us, is released into the world.

If this sounds familiar, there is a good reason. It's the Great Commandment, the pattern in which Jesus tells us to order our lives. Let's take a deeper look. In the Gospels of Matthew and Mark, a question is posed to Jesus. In Matthew, a Pharisee asks Jesus a question to test him.

"Teacher, which is the most important commandment in the law of Moses?" (Matt. 22:36). The Gospel of Mark, in a scene that seems a bit less hostile, reports one of the scribes asking, "Which commandment is the first of all?" (Mark 12:28 NRSV). This question itself is not unusual. As the scribes and Pharisees made rules and regulations the center of their religious life, it should come as no surprise that this question was often debated in rabbinic schools. It probably came up many times among those listening to Jesus. Now, he is being asked to choose the single most important commandment from among more than six hundred commandments in the Torah.

Jesus begins his reply with an answer that would find general agreement among his questioners, beginning in Mark with the Shema ("Hear, O Israel"), the centerpiece of a Jewish prayer service. To the traditional wording (Deut. 6:4) he added a fourth source ("mind") for wholehearted love of God. "The first is, 'Hear, O Israel: the Lord our God, the Lord is one; you shall love the Lord your God with all your heart, and with all your soul, and with all your mind, and with all your strength'" (Mark 12:29–30 NRSV). Then Jesus continued, beyond the expectation of the questioner. At first the agenda was set by the questioner, now Jesus owns the agenda. As he did in so much of his ministry, Jesus was moving the conversation to a deeper and ever so much more important message.

Jesus drew from a less frequently quoted command from the Old Testament: "Do not seek revenge or bear a grudge against a fellow Israelite, but love your neighbor as yourself. I am the Lord" (Lev. 19:18). As Jesus put the command, "The second is this, 'You shall love your neighbor as yourself.' There is no other commandment greater than these" (Mark 12:31 NRSV). We need to adjust our normal understanding of order here. Jesus isn't so much starting a list of commandments, number one, number two, etc. He is giving a full and complete answer to the question. While the command to love God importantly comes first, we are also to understand that either commandment alone would fall short of conveying the full truth. Each has its completion in the other. We do love God first, but it must not stop there. It continues to the love of neighbor. We do love our neighbor, but it is our fulfilling relationship of mutual love with God that makes this possible. The only way a person can prove that he or she loves God is by showing that love to others.

Note another very important change from the command as it is found in Leviticus. There the limits of the command to love were set in terms of "a fellow Israelite" or "your kin" or "your relative" or "your brother" in various translations. It certainly did not include Gentiles. In fact, it was okay to hate Gentiles. Jesus allows no such limitation. The concept of neighbor was extended to even include our enemies (Matt. 5:44). Jesus took an old law and gave it new meaning.

The conversation continued with Jesus saying in Matthew, "The entire law and all the demands of the prophets are based on these two commandments" (22:40). In Mark, the scribe recognizes the truth in what Jesus is saying and adds, "This is more important than to offer all of the burnt offerings and sacrifices required in the law" (12:33). What a remarkable revelation! The law and the Prophets held the essentials of the Jewish religion. Sacrifices in the temple were at the very center of Jewish life, but these two commands are greater. Again, Jesus is pointing to a broader truth. The underlying assumption is that

> there is some principle upon which the individual commandments of the Torah and the words of the prophets depend for their ultimate origins and validity. It is not a question of which commandment is the greatest or the first to which it speaks, but a question as to what is the basis on which the "law and the prophets" are to be considered as proceeding in their particularity.[3]

This leads to the understanding that "the whole law and prophets can be exegetically deduced from the command to love God and neighbor."[4] Simply put, every truth in the law and the prophets flows from love of God and love of neighbor.

How do we implement this love in our life in community today? This is our command, our guiding principle. The God of love has created us for his purpose, exquisitely found in loving God and loving our fellow human beings. Together these commands are a basis upon which we as disciples of Jesus are to order our lives. Sounds simple, but we all know it isn't. It's quite easy to say this is what we should do, but the question remains, How do we accomplish this? This reorientation is resisted by those instincts or character traits that arose with the fall.

The reasons for not doing what we know we ought to do are probably infinite, but certainly many of them are rooted in selfishness and insecurity, in attempts to establish our own worth. I need my money or power over others or fame or what have you as ways of demonstrating, not only to others but also, and perhaps primarily, to myself, that I am a real and valuable person, a force to be reckoned with. If I become free of this need, if I become convinced that I am already valued regardless of my own achievements or lack of them, the sacrifices necessary to fulfillment of my moral obligations will be easier to make. "Rather than being the source of harsh moral demands, God's love makes it possible, or at least makes it easier, for me to fulfill whatever moral duties or desires I already have."[5]

Jesus knows how difficult it is for us to love our neighbor. So we are not left on our own. The relationships envisioned in the Great Commandment are impossible except as God does a supernatural work in us. How does God equip us to obey this command? It bears repeating that this process is primarily a profound and mysterious work of the Holy Spirit. Our deepest need is to return to God as the center of our being. We align ourselves with the Holy Spirit by faith and agree as the Holy Spirit uses our prayers, Bible study, worship, fellowship, etc., to give us the desire and power to please God (Phil. 2:13). This is spiritual formation, a radical reorientation of who we are and how we see other people.

The gospel is not merely a message of intellectual assent to a doctrine or a formula for getting to heaven. It is stepping into a relationship with a living Person who embraces us in a whole new way of being. Spiritual formation is growth in the self-giving image of God. Much more than merely a call to right doing, restoration of the image in which humankind was created is about right being. So right being is not simply a reordering of activities; it is a reordering of relationship. The incredible revelation of Scripture is that in right being we find true freedom in the presence of God, the abiding of which Jesus speaks in John 15, abiding in the "perichoretic"* intimacy of the "Son and the Father in the Spirit."[6]

Trusting that we are part of this intimate relationship and letting it live through us is a life change that demands courageous faith, a faith that allows us to surrender our rights. Then our true nature as designed by God begins to respond to God. There is nothing more natural than desiring to protect and insist upon our rights, but if we are graced with a life of courageous faith, we have the increasing ability to waive our rights for the sake of God's best for others. "Freedom is found when we are able to get outside of ourselves and live for the other."[7] This is fiercely resisted by our fallen nature. In *The Deeper Journey*, Robert Mulholland examines the fallen nature, or in his terms the false self, and how it can actually hold us hostage. He writes, "[Jeremiah] reveals there are two fundamental ways of being human in the world; trusting in our human resources and abilities or a radical trust in God."[8] The orientation of one's heart is a watershed. How we live in community will turn on the orientation of the self, whether oriented to God for the sake of others or to self for the

---

*A concept that expresses the intimacy of the triune God. The Father, Son, and Holy Spirit not only embrace each other, they also permeate each other and dwell in each other in an insepa-rable oneness.

sake of self. This, of course, is not an all-or-nothing, static way of being. It is a lifelong process in which a person may modulate between the two orientations in many varied situations encountered on a daily basis.

The essence of the false self is surrender to the temptation to take over God's role in our lives. Simply put, we place our trust in ourselves rather than in God, in our sufficiency rather than God's sufficiency. This is the malady of all despite having been created to have true life (identity, meaning, value, and purpose) flow from loving union with God to the deepest part of our being (John 17:20–23). We fear being unacceptable and unlovable, so we seek to find our fullness and our affirmation in various sources we select other than God. We place our trust in those other sources.

Consider a few of the traits of the false self as described by Mulholland. The first is that the false self is a fearful self. Dependence on self means we sink our identity into and draw our meaning, value, and purpose from what we do, what we achieve, and how we perform. Our fearful self, relying on this foundation, fears that we might not be valued according to our expectations. We depend on our own criteria to provide affirmation. But others may not give due regard to our performance, or they may outperform us and thereby diminish the efficacy of our performance and prove our foundation to be inadequate. The false self becomes fearful of both our ability to establish our own value and the danger that our perceived value will be diminished by others.

> As our false self manages our life, we fear that we might not be valued. If our false self's identity is rooted in our performance, then our value must

> necessarily be rooted in how well we perform. Consequently, our false self attempts to perfect our performance, at least in our own estimation if not in the estimation of others. . . . All that matters is that our performance achieve that measure of success that provides our false self with the necessary affirmation of our value.[9]

Other flaws of the false self follow closely. If others interfere in some way with the feedback we expect from our self-established criteria on which we rely for our affirmation, that interference is fertile ground for anger. As we depend more and more on these resources (relationships, material resources, and intellectual and informational assets), we become protective of them as the source of our affirmation and defensive against anything perceived as attacking them. We sink our identity into who we know, what we have, and what we know, which enhances our distorted image of self, and we become self-promoting, always promoting ourselves and our agenda. The problem is, none of these criteria used by the false self for its affirmation were ever intended to "bear the weight of our identity as children of God. God alone is capable of bearing the weight of our identity."[10]

Our fallen self always wants to be vindicated. Recognizing the harm that accompanies self-vindication, Saint Augustine prayed, "O Lord, deliver me from this lust of always vindicating myself." Such a need for constant vindication destroys our soul's faith in God. It stands in opposition to our ability to ask in any situation how we might love God and neighbor. When the false self is listening to distorted input, the adverse impact on relationships readily follows. The desire to receive honor as a way of self-satisfaction is an example of distorted input. Spiritual leaders have explored the idea of a believer learning to live without such dependence. Andrew Murray writes:

> Brethren! Nothing can cure you of the desire to receive honor from men, or of the sensitivity and pain and anger which come when it is not given, except giving yourself to seek only the glory that comes from God. *Let the glory of the all-glorious God be everything to you.* You will be freed from the glory of men and of self, and be content and glad to be nothing. Out of this nothingness you will grow strong in faith, giving glory to God. *You will find that the deeper you sink in humility before Him, the nearer He is to fulfill every desire of your faith.*[11]

On this concept of *nothingness* Paul writes that Jesus made himself nothing, taking on the humble station of one serving in human form (Phil. 2:7). Paul also writes of his own experience, surrendering a position of high esteem according to the religious values of Judaism for a life in which all the things of the world, those things perceived to give value such as education, achievement, and status, became worthless to him *when compared to* the priceless value of knowing Jesus as Lord (Phil. 3:8). For Paul, life in Christ became totally sufficient, not just as a slogan but in reality. We note parenthetically that Paul continued to use his intellect and education, achieved what few others would even dream of, and has the status of one used mightily by God to establish the Christian faith. But even in this, Paul's value came from his relationship with Jesus.

Thomas à Kempis wrote about nothingness and knew it was a key to overcoming malice from others. When honor is sought, the opinions of others gain exaggerated importance. Remember hearing the adage, "Words can never harm you"? They are only words, yet when used to slight they take on enormous power, "because you still have a worldly outlook and pay more attention to others' opinions than you should."[12] Jumping forward many centuries, Dallas Willard writes, "Why should we worry about others' opinions of us when God is for us and Jesus Christ is on his right hand pleading our interests (Rom. 8:31–34)? But we do."[13] The limitation lies in the ability of the believer to fully trust in God's sufficiency.

Performance, possessions, vindication, and honor are about approval, but approval from where? The true sign that one is right with God is a changed heart produced by the Holy Spirit. A person with this changed heart seeks approval from God, not praise from people. The changed heart is one that is more oriented toward God, more trusting in God. Pointedly, this passage does not say such a person does not seek approval; rather, it says approval is sought from God. It does not say the need for affirmation is eliminated, rather the need is met by an approval that may be multifaceted but has its source in God. God's approval is adequate, and even more. When approval is sought from God, it is sought through trust in the true source of one's self. It is good to want to please God. For the believer to know that God is pleased with her and that she is a beloved child is a place of well-being. "True freedom comes when we no longer need to be somebody special in other people's eyes because we know we are loveable and good enough."[14]

Such high standards! We can understand why we have to rely on God to move us toward them. The success of a disciple of Jesus in turning to God for the satisfaction of God-given needs is in direct proportion to the extent to which the believer is able to trust in God. This trust has always been our calling, a courageous faith that forsakes dependence on easy but false sources of identity, approval, and honor, and instead looks to God. All humanity, with the exception of that humanity in Jesus, has had a fallen nature that would rather trust in its own way, chart its own course, than place trust in God. This may be the most distinctive feature of the fallen world. This failure of trust was initiated by Adam and Eve through their original sin in the first garden, the garden of Eden. On the other hand, perfect trust was demonstrated by Jesus throughout his life reaching its climax in the second garden, the garden of Gethsemane, where he surrendered totally to the will of the Father.

Without minimizing its complexity, it is a simple truth that spiritual formation is inseparable from the reestablishment of trust in God. It sounds so simple. In principle it is. Just trust God. Yet this is a lifelong challenge for most. Every challenge faced in life presents an opportunity to deepen trust, our casual conviction becoming courageous faith. The fallen nature will always place trust in inadequate sources. In community we may learn that the ability to surrender rights for the good of others is the measure of one's response to Jesus' command to love one's neighbor. How is it possible to do this as an act of joyful service? Rights may be truly surrendered for the sake of others only when the overflowing sufficiency of God is realized. When a right is surrendered, it creates a void. The acceptance and approval of our Father are perfect for filling that void. "We are able to give up our *being* for others because our life is in the Spirit, 'hidden with Christ in God' (Col. 3:3), which is the only place in which we can really be free, delighting in the infinitely shared pleasure of the beautiful life of God."[15]

The crowd around the cross mocked Jesus, shouting that he should save himself. They jeered, "If you are the Son of God, save yourself and come down from the cross!" (Matt. 27:40). Picture the scene. At that moment, naked and dying as a criminal, what did Jesus have? He had surrendered his rights for the sake of others. He was nothing by human standards. But as one valued by God and whose value comes from God, he never for an instant gave up his status as the beloved Son, one in whom the Father is well pleased. The Jewish and Roman leaders mocked Jesus, beat him, and hung him on a cross to die a criminal's death. The one thing they did not and could not do was diminish who he was, the beloved Son of God. His trust that his value was eternally secure in the Father enabled him to surrender all.

The abrasions of community can be used as means of grace. "Accept every humiliation, look upon every fellow-man who tries or vexes you, as a means of grace to humble you. Use every opportunity to humble yourself before your fellow-men as a help to remain humble before God."[16] This is surely one of the most challenging disciplines of spiritual formation. Dennis Kinlaw writes, "How do you get to this place of absolute freedom, where Jesus can do with you whatever He wills? Recognize that the One who holds you in the palm of His hand is greater than any force in the world. When He matters more to you than any other thing does, even life itself, then you are free."[17] This calls for courageous faith that accepts that God's purpose for us in this life is not about ease and comfort, but being molded as children who will spend the rest of eternity in the presence of the Holy Trinity.

Serious engagement in spiritual formation causes one to understand how deep, intense, and difficult the command is to love your neighbor as yourself. If true love of self is found in worth that comes from God, the believer is to love others as people whose worth comes from God as well. Progress in this transformation may be slow. It's a place in which an assurance of the unfailing love of God is critical. Our image of God must be a true image. How unfortunate that even among believers today, the image of God is distorted. For some, the image of God is of a stern taskmaster sitting in judgment, waiting to condemn for our slightest misstep, compelling us to conform to some legalistic list. For others, the image of God has been watered down to a benevolent spirit in the sky who really just wants us to feel good about ourselves and is happy with us just the way we are. Both of these are distorted and contribute to a disbelief that God really loves us wholeheartedly, urging us on when we fall short and celebrating even our small victories with joy. Beloved, God cares deeply, and is not glaring at our failures when we are seeking to live a holy life in community. The image of God must be and the true image of him is that of a Father and friend rejoicing in the victories, large and small, and urging his beloved children on toward the next victory. "So now we can rejoice in our wonderful new relationship with God because our Lord Jesus Christ has made us friends of God" (Rom. 5:11).

Through his letter to the Colossians, Paul is saying to us today that now that we have become children of our heavenly Father, we should look to our Father and his promises for who we are and how this new life is affirmed (Col. 3:1). Set your sights on heaven, the place where the love of God is complete and sufficient. To do this requires that the Holy Spirit lead the believer to embrace the superiority of a life of trust in the sufficiency of God as our guiding certainty. Then our fullness, our affirmation, comes not from criteria we have established but from God. "God has planted Christ as the seed of a true life in loving union with God."[18] As little by little we are shown that we don't need to depend on the things to which our false self clings, we can release them. We begin to have the mind of Christ (1 Cor. 2:16). It is in this freedom from the false self and its crutches that we find the freedom to begin to live out the Great Commandment, loving God for the sake of others. "In our relationship with God through Jesus Christ we are made whole, indeed, and therefore freed to love with our whole selves."[19] Freedom is the ability to not do what pleases me but do what is pleasing to God.

Sometimes it seems like I have been writing in a place separate from the world where I can think, *What a marvelous life God has prepared for us!* Then I reenter the world and wonder if what I have written is just an illusion, an unachievable dream. I'm convinced that it is not, that it is true. For one thing, I don't doubt the love of God, his desire to mold his children, and the power of the indwelling Holy Spirit. Added to that, I have seen and heard of great change in others and experienced change myself. God's image and design for us, reiterated by Jesus in the Great Commandment, and empowered by the giving of the Holy Spirit, is teaching us to ask in any circumstance how we are to love God and neighbor. We grow so this is becoming our first thought, not an afterthought. "Humanly speaking, it is impossible. But with God everything is possible" (Matt. 19:26).

As Joshua faced Jericho, he was encouraged to be bold and to act with courageous faith. The enemy was formidable, but he was confident in the command of God, knew of God's work throughout the history of Israel, and was backed by a powerful, successful army. But perhaps his greater expression of courageous faith came in later years, when Israel was being tempted by the pagan tribes surrounding them to abandon God and adopt pagan practices. It seems that Joshua was facing the most difficult form of opposition, that which came from within Israel. With military victories and conquest of the land now in the past, Joshua still summoned courageous faith as he spoke to the nation: "Choose today whom you will serve. Would you prefer the gods your ancestors served beyond the Euphrates? Or will it be the gods of the Amorites in whose land you now live? But as for me and my family, we will serve the LORD" (Josh. 24:15). Courageous faith! Choose this day whom you will serve.

Reflection and Application

1. Does the Great Commandment deserve a position of prominence in your life and in your relationships? Why? Is it guiding and transforming your life as it should? Does it need to be given more prominence? If so, how might this happen?

2. Put in your own words how freedom can come from a surrender of your rights.

3. The "sufficiency of God" is a big, broad phrase. Name some of your needs in which God is or can be sufficient. Describe that sufficiency; what does/would it look like?

4. Does your image of God help or hinder your ability to live in courageous faith? How does that image affect how you live out your life as a follower of Jesus? Are there ways in which your image of God as Father needs to be corrected?

5. Reflect prayerfully on some of the areas mentioned in this chapter (self-vindication, approval, possessions, surrender, etc.) asking that God give you the desire and the power to please him.

6. What is one thought you can take from this chapter to reflect upon in the days ahead with the guidance of the Holy Spirit? What is one prayer over which you will spend time with the Lord?

Notes

Chapter 1: Setting Our Sights on Heaven

1. William Barclay, *The Letter to the Hebrews*, The Daily Study Bible Series, rev. ed. (Philadelphia: Westminster, 1976), 120.
2. C. S. Lewis, *The Screwtape Letters* (New York: MacMillan, 1961), 10.
3. J. C. Ryle, *Holiness: Its Nature, Hindrances, Difficulties, and Roots* (Hertfordshire: Evangelical Press, 1879), 22.
4. C. S. Lewis, *The Weight of Glory* (New York: Macmillan, 1949), 26.
5. Keith Meyer, "Whole-Life Transformation," in ed. Alan Andrews, *The Kingdom Life: A Practical Theology of Discipleship and Spiritual Formation* (Colorado Springs: NavPress, 2010), 144.

Chapter 2: The Mistake of the Pharisees

1. Steve DeNeff, *The Way of Holiness: Experience God's Work in You* (Indianapolis: Wesleyan, 2010), 153.
2. Alice Camille, "Outward Signs," *U.S. Catholic* (September 2000), 44.
3. Stephanie Harrison, "The Case of the Pharisee and the Tax Collector: Justification and Social Location in Luke's Gospel," *Currents in Theology and Mission*, 32.2 (April 2005), 100–01.

4. Joel Green, *The New International Commentary on the New Testament: The Gospel of Luke* (Grand Rapids: Eerdmans, 1997), 647.
5. Frederick C. Holmgren, "The Pharisee and the Tax Collector: Luke 18:9–14 and Deuteronomy 26:1–15," *Interpretation: A Journal of Bible & Theology* (July 1994, vol. 48, issue 3), 252–61, 255.
6. Larry Osborne, *Accidental Pharisees: Avoiding Pride, Exclusivity, and the Other Dangers of Overzealous Faith* (Grand Rapids: Zondervan, 2012), 24.
7. Harrison, "The Case of the Pharisee and the Tax Collector," 109.
8. Ibid., 103.
9. Michael W. Mangis, *Signature Sins: Taming Our Wayward Hearts* (Downers Grove, IL: InterVarsity, 2008), 53.
10. Oswald Chambers, *My Utmost for His Highest: Updated Edition in Today's Language,* ed. James Reimann (Grand Rapids, MI: Discovery House Publishers, 1992), November 23.
11. John J. Kilgallen, SJ, SSD, *The Pharisee and the Publican (Luke 18:9–14): The Point?* (*The Expository Times*, Feb. 2003, vol. 114, issue 5): 157–59.
12. William Barclay, *The Daily Study Bible Series: The Gospel of Luke* (Philadelphia: Westminster, 1975), 225.
13. Osborne, *Accidental Pharisees*, 25.
14. Richard F. Lovelace, *Renewal as a Way of Life: A Guidebook for Spiritual Growth* (Eugene, OR: Wipf, 2002), 18–19, emphasis added.
15. Chambers, *My Utmost for His Highest*, 9.

Chapter 3: Dry Seasons

1. Oswald Chambers, *My Utmost for His Highest: Updated Edition in Today's Language,* ed. James Reimann (Grand

Rapids, MI: Discovery House Publishers, 1992), October 13.

2. Lewis J. Stulman, "Jeremiah as a Messenger of Hope in Crisis," *Interpretation*, 62, no. 1. (January 2008), 5–20, 7.
3. Thomas à Kempis, *The Imitation of Christ in Four Books: A Translation from the Latin*, rev. ed., ed. Joseph N. Tylenda (New York: Vintage, 1998), 122.
4. Francis de Sales, *Introduction to the Devout Life*, trans. John K. Ryan (New York: Image, 1989), 92.
5. Brother Lawrence, *Practicing the Presence of God: A Modernized Christian Classic*. eds. Robert J. Edmonson and Tony Jones (Brewster: Paraclete, 2007), 45.
6. Andrew D. Lester, "Why Hast Thou Forsaken Me! Anger at God," *Journal of Pastoral Theology*, 16, no. 2 (Fall 2006), 53–70, 54.
7. Frederick C. Holmgren, "The Elusive Presence: Jeremiah 20:4–11," *Currents in Theology and Mission*, 33, no. 5 (October 2006), 366–71, 371.

Chapter 4: The Problem of Suffering

1. Fredrick J. Gaiser, "'Your Sins Are Forgiven . . . Stand Up and Walk': A Theological Reading of Mark 2:1–12 in the Light of Psalm 103," *Ex Auditu*, 21 2005, 78.
2. Walter J. Ciszek and Daniel L. Flaherty, *He Leadeth Me: An Extraordinary Testament of Faith* (San Francisco: Ignatius Press, 1995), 20.
3. Thomas à Kempis, *The Imitation of Christ in Four Books: A Translation from the Latin*, rev. ed. Joseph N. Tylenda (New York: Vintage, 1998), 51.
4. Andrew Murray, *Humility* (Springdale, PA: Whitaker House, 1982), 81.
5. Gordon T. Smith, *The Voice of Jesus: Discernment, Prayer, and the Witness of the Spirit* (Downers Grove, IL: InterVarsity, 2003), 84.

6. Oswald Chambers, *My Utmost for His Highest: Updated Edition in Today's Language*, ed. James Reimann (Grand Rapids, MI: Discovery House, 1992), February 1.
7. Peggy Reynoso, "Formed through Suffering," in Alan Andrews, ed. *The Kingdom Life: A Practical Theology of Discipleship and Spiritual Formation* (Colorado Springs: NavPress, 2010), 178.
8. Ibid., 163.
9. Ibid., 177.
10. Paul E. Billheimer, *Don't Waste Your Sorrows: New Insight into God's Eternal Purpose for Each Christian in the Midst of Life's Greatest Adversities* (Minneapolis: Bethany House, 1977), 78.
11. Ibid., 118.
12. Thomas à Kempis, *The Imitation of Christ in Four Books: A Translation from the Latin*. rev. ed. ed. Joseph N. Tylenda (New York: Vintage, 1998), 15.
13. Smith, *The Voice of Jesus*, 84.
14. Michael W. Mangis, *Signature Sins: Taming Our Wayward Hearts* (Downers Grove, IL: InterVarsity, 2008), 261.
15. Reynoso, "Formed through Suffering," 174.
16. https://outreachmagazine.com/interviews/22041-krish-kandiah-2.html/2, accessed July 2, 2019.
17. Reynoso, "Formed through Suffering," 186.
18. Mrs. Charles E. Cowman, *Streams in the Desert* (Grand Rapids: Zondervan, 1925, 1965), April 1st.
19. Billheimer, *Don't Waste Your Sorrows*, 35.

Chapter 5: Forgiven

1. Thomas C. Oden, *The Living God: Systematic Theology: Volume One* (HarperSanFrancisco, 1987), 100.
2. Ibid., 111.
3. Ibid., 111.
4. Ibid., 116.

5. Ibid., 118.
6. G. E. Ladd, "God the Father: New Testament," *The International Standard Bible Encyclopedia*, revised, Geoffrey W. Bromiley, ed. (Grand Rapids: Eerdmans, 1982), 510.
7. Joachim Jeremias, *New Testament Theology: Proclamation of Jesus* (New York: Scribner, 1971), 66.
8. G. E. Ladd, "God the Father: New Testament," 510–11.
9. Tim L. Anderson, "God Our Father as a Script of Intimacy for Those Suffering Shame," *Journal of Spiritual Formation & Soul Care* (2016, vol. 2), 247–69.
10. Brennan Manning, *The Relentless Tenderness of Jesus* (Grand Rapids: Chosen Books, 1986), 24.
11. Dennis F. Kinlaw, *This Day with the Master: 365 Daily Meditations* (Grand Rapids: Zondervan, 2002), July 29.
12. David G. Benner, *The Gift of Being Yourself: The Sacred Call to Self-Discovery* (Downers Grove, IL: InterVarsity Press, 2004), 67.
13. James Byron Smith, *The Good and Beautiful God* (Downers Grove, IL: IVP Books, 2009), 96.
14. Mark E. Biddle, "Genesis 3: Sin, Shame and Self-Esteem," *Review and Expositor* (103, Spring 2006), 363.
15. Leanna K. Fuller, "Perfectionism and Shame: Exploring the Connections," *The Journal of Pastoral Theology* (vol. 18, no.1, Summer 2008), 47.
16. Asa Sphar, "A Theology of Shame as Revealed in the Creation Story," *The Theological Educator*, Spring 1997 (55): 68–69.
17. Margaret B. Hess, "A Portrait of Shame," *Christian Century* (May 21–28, 1997), 509.
18. Henri J. M. Nouwen, *The Return of the Prodigal Son: A Story of Homecoming* (New York: Doubleday, 1992), 52.
19. Ibid., 37.
20. Benner, *The Gift of Being Yourself*, 35.
21. Ibid., 60.

Chapter 6: Forgiving

1. David, Augsburger, *The New Freedom of Forgiveness,* 3rd ed. (Chicago: Moody, 2000), 20.
2. *60 Minutes*, "The Most Unlikely Meeting," May 12, 2019.
3. William Barclay, *The Gospel of Mark*, The Daily Study Bible Series, rev. ed. (Philadelphia: Westminster, 1976), 51.
4. Jesse Couenhoven, "Forgiveness and Restoration: A Theological Exploration," *Journal of Religion* 90.2 (2010), 148–70, 158.
5. Miroslav Volf, *Free of Charge: Giving and Forgiving in a Culture Stripped of Grace* (Grand Rapids: Zondervan, 2005), 129.
6. Couenhoven, "Forgiveness and Restoration," 163.
7. Ibid., 163.
8. Augsburger, *The New Freedom of Forgiveness*, 25.
9. Volf, *Free of Charge*, 161.
10. Dennis F. Kinlaw, *This Day with the Master: 365 Daily Meditations* (Grand Rapids: Zondervan, 2002), May 8.
11. Asa Sphar, "A Theology of Shame as Revealed in the Creation Story," *The Theological Educator* Spring 1997(55): 64–74, 73.
12. Laura Hillenbrand, *Unbroken: A World War II Story of Survival, Resilience, and Redemption* (New York: Random House, 2010).
13. https://www.guideposts.org/inspiration/stories-of-hope/guideposts-classics-corrie-ten-boom-on-forgiveness?nopaging=1 accessed, April 11, 2019.
14. Martha E. Stortz, "The Practice of Forgiveness: Disciples as Forgiven Forgivers," *Word & World*, vol. 27, no. 1 (Winter 2007), 21.
15. John Henry Jowett, *A Daily Meditation,* revised by Graham and Carol Houghton, South Asian Institute of Advanced Christian Studies (Bangalore, 2005), February 13.

16. Brad A. Binau, "'Holding On' and 'Letting Go': The Dynamics of Forgiveness," *Word & World*, vol. 27, no. 1 (Winter 2007): 23–31, 30.

Chapter 7: Courageous Faith in Community

1. Michael W. Mangis, *Signature Sins: Taming Our Wayward Hearts* (Downers Grove, IL: InterVarsity, 2008), 165.
2. F. Leron Shults and Steven J. Sandage, *Transforming Spirituality: Integrating Theology and Psychology* (Grand Rapids: Baker Academic, 2006), 143.
3. Arland J. Hultgren, "The Double Commandment of Love in MT 22:34–40: Its Sources and Composition," *The Catholic Biblical Quarterly* (36 no. 3 July 1974), 373–78, 377.
4. Brice L. Martin, "Matthew on Christ and the Law," *Theological Studies* (Mar. 83, vol. 44, issue 1), 53–70, 63.
5. Donald F. Dreisbach, "On the Love of God," *Anglican Theological Review* (59 no. 1 Jan. 1977), 32–43, 43.
6. Shults and Sandage, *Transforming Spirituality,* 145.
7. Fredrick J. Gaiser, "'Your Sins Are Forgiven . . . Stand up and Walk': A Theological Reading of Mark 2:1–12 in the Light of Psalm 103," *Ex Auditu*, (21 2005), 71–87, 73.
8. M. Robert Mulholland Jr., *The Deeper Journey: The Spirituality of Discovering Your True Self* (Downers Grove, IL: IVP Books, 2016), 23.
9. Ibid., 32.
10. Ibid., 31.
11. Andrew Murray, *Humility* (Springdale, PA: Whitaker House, 1982), 72, emphasis added.
12. Thomas à Kempis, *The Imitation of Christ in Four Books: A Translation from the Latin*. rev. ed. ed. Joseph N. Tylenda (New York: Vintage, 1998), 145.

13. Dallas Willard, *The Spirit of the Disciplines: Understanding How God Changes Lives* (San Francisco: Harper, 1988), 165.
14. Peter Scazzero, *Emotionally Healthy Spirituality* (Grand Rapids: Zondervan, 2006), 77.
15. Shults and Sandage, *Transforming Spirituality,* 146.
16. Murray, *Humility,* 75.
17. Dennis F. Kinlaw, *The Mind of Christ* (Nappanee, IN: Francis Asbury, 1998), August 31.
18. Mulholland, *The Deeper Journey,* 86.
19. Agnes W. Norfleet, "Between Text and Sermon," *Interpretation* (51 No. 4, Oct. 1997), 403–06, 406.

CPSIA information can be obtained
at www.ICGtesting.com
Printed in the USA
LVHW010431060821
693986LV00004B/14

9 781628 247664